LONDON

AT

WAR

Rescue workers, nurses, police, firemen and passers by all lend a hand in
Glasshouse Street following a V1 rocket attack, June 1944.

Clive Hardy & Nigel Arthur

First published 1989 by
Quoin Publishing Ltd
The Barn
36A North Road
Kirkburton
Huddersfield HD8 0RH

in association with

The Hulton-Deutsch Ltd Collection
Unique House
21-23 Woodfield Road
London W9 2BA

Typesetting and reproduction by
Airegraphic Ltd
17-18 Enterprise Park, Old Lane, Beeston
Leeds LS11 8HA.

Printed and bound by
Netherwood Dalton Co Ltd
Caxton Works
Bradley Mill
Huddersfield

ISBN 1 85563 006 0

Designed by Clive Hardy
Cover painting by Denise Jackson-Moore

The first day of rationing in January 1940.

Introduction & Acknowledgements

"We have nearly twenty five million images in here," said Peter Elliott as he gave Nick Netherwood of Quóin Publishing and myself a conducted tour of the Hulton-Deutsch Collection. We had come down to meet Peter, the Managing Director, to discuss the possibility of compiling this book using material drawn almost exclusively from the collection, and of making sure that it was published in time for the fiftieth anniversary of the outbreak of the war, for time alas was not on our side.

There was one drawback; Nick and I, like Peter, are fascinated by photographs and being allowed into areas where there are thousands of boxes each containing scores of photographs was almost too much. Opening each box was like unwrapping a mystery present on Christmas morning; one knows there's something in there, but just what remains a suprise to the very last moment.

The main problem was to structure the content of the book so that it would portray reasonably accurately and fairly the experiences of the men, women and children of London during the Second World War. The book could not be and is not a definitive blow by blow account of those years, but it is an attempt to recapture the atmosphere of the period, when this country fought for its very survival against a determined enemy in a war which directly affected the lives of everyone, male or female, young or old, rich or poor.

As well as looking at everyday life in the capital, which was forced to adapt to the stringent demands of war with the rationing of food, fuel and clothing, there are sections devoted to civil defence, the Home Guard, the Blitz and so on. The photographs have been specially processed using computer enhancement techniques, which should, if we've done our job properly, give them a depth and clarity not seen before — take a very leisurely stroll through these pages, using a magnifying glass where necessary, to discover the many treasures that lie waiting. Welcome to the dramatic, humorous, magnificent, sad, courageous and gripping world of the war years, in pictures.

I should like to take this opportunity of thanking Peter Elliott and his colleagues for their help, Nigel Arthur for rushing pen in hand to our aid, John Netherwood for helping the project off the ground in the first place, Denise Jackson-Moore for the magnificent cover painting which is based on the famous *Daily Mail* photograph taken by Herbert Mason, and the staff of Netherwood Dalton for their fine workmanship and technical expertise in printing and binding *London at War*.

For those of you, who after looking through *London at War* would like more detailed reads, there are several books to choose from. *The People's War* by Angus Calder, published by Granada, is perhaps the best book ever written on the Home Front. *Firemen at War* by Neil Wallington, published by David & Charles, covers the work of London's firefighters. For the bombing, the *pièce de résistance* is *The Blitz Then and Now* which is published in several volumes by Battle of Britain Prints International, and is jam packed full of information and photographs.

So, enough of my chat — good reading and searching.

Clive Hardy
August 1989

The Ministry of Supply's Home Guard gets to grips with Lewis Gun MKIIIs. March 1941.

The Road to War

The Treaty of Versailles had placed the responsibility for the outbreak of the First World War upon Germany and her Allies. Under the terms of the treaty Germany was virtually disarmed. She was relieved of her overseas possessions, and the provinces of Alsace-Lorrain were ceded to France. Eupen and Malmedy were given to Belgium, Poland was given West Prussia and Posen, and Memel Danzig and the Saar were placed under military occupation. Her industries were stripped of machinery and equipment, many of her merchant ships were requisitioned and even railway locomotives were taken, partly to meet reparations assessed at 136,000 million gold marks, but also to make her suffer. Of the treaty Marshal Foch said "This is not peace, it is an armistice for twenty years" He was right.

Of Germany's former Allies, the once mighty Austria-Hungarian Empire came off worst. The empire had collapsed into anarchy before the end of the war. The central Hapsburg Government, which had for so long held together in uneasy companionship Serbs, Magyars, Austrians, Slovaks and a score of minority races, ceased to function. The result was that the empire split up into a number of successor states who then began to squabble amongst themselves over the position of new frontiers. Things were so bad that many people simply did not know which 'new' country they belonged to. Numerous army units simply disbanded there was no one, or anywhere, to go to officially demobilise.

It was hoped that the external politics of states would in future be settled by a new organisation, the League of Nations. The League had been set up specifically to promote international peace through collective security. Unhappily the League failed. On a number of occasions the Assembly dithered and any pretences of a collective security system were shredded in September 1931 when Japan invaded, with impunity, China's northern province, Manchuria.

In December 1934, a frontier dispute at Wal Wal on the Abyssinia/Italian Somaliland border, was used by the Italians as a pretext to pour troops, tanks and artillery into their colony. For ten months, Abyssinia appealed to the League to arbitrate. On 3rd October the Italians invaded. In November economic and financial sanctions were half-heartedly imposed on Italy. A month later, Sir Samuel Hoare, Foreign Secretary, met with his French opposite number Pierre Laval and concocted a plan whereby two-thirds of Abyssinia would be handed over to the Italians in the name of appeasement. *The Times*, usually a supporter of appeasement, denounced the proposals and Baldwin, albeit temporarily, sacked Hoare to save his own political neck. At the end of April 1936, Emperor Haile Selassie made his final appeal to the League for help. "I must still hold on until my tardy Allies appear, and if they never come then I say prophetically and without bitterness, the West will perish." A week later, Italian troops entered Selassie's capital Addis Ababa. The emperor fled into exile and Italy formally announced the annexation of Abyssinia.

In Britain and America.

In October 1929, a brand new luxury apartment on New York's plush Fifth Avenue cost around 1,500 dollars a week to rent and a ticket to one of the hit Broadway shows averaged out at 28 dollars. By the end of November, the Fifth Avenue rental had been slashed to 150 dollars a week and theatre tickets were down in price to 2-3 dollars each. The financial crisis at the New York Stock Exchange had started to bite.

American industry had grown rapidly since the end of the Great War due to a deliberate policy of readily available loans from the Federal Reserve Bank. In Europe, United States loans between 1925-29 amounted to a staggering 2,900 million dollars, and some countries including Britain were suffering from overseas competition for their traditional industries, whereas others including Czechoslovakia, Austria, and Germany were enjoying a period of relative prosperity. In July 1929, the supply of goods in the United States finally outstripped demand, necessitating a reduction in output and massive redundancies. Investors began to lose confidence and substantial losses on share prices occurred. By the end of October, 18,000 million dollars had been wiped off the value of shares. The Wall Street Crash, however, had only just begun, for though a modest recovery was made during the first months of 1930, by June, the market was once again on a downward slide which would last unabated for twenty-five months. By July 1932, the value of all stocks listed on Wall Street shrank from 90,000 million dollars to just under 16,000 million and the effect was worldwide.

In 1931 Europe was rocked by a banking crisis with the collapse of the Vienna Bank in Austria and a run on the German Reichsbank. Severe financial strain was placed on London and the Labour Government, already battling against the slump and a dole queue of two million, was incapable of putting together a programme of economic measures. The Government resigned and Ramsey MacDonald, together with a handful of Labour MP's, joined forces with the Conservatives to form a 'National' Government. One of Labour's more able members, Sir Oswald Moseley, Chancellor of the Duchy of Lancaster, had already left the Government because the Cabinet had failed to support his scheme to bring down unemployment with a programme of public works, a higher school leaving age, early retirement, and the control of credit through the banks. Moseley and his followers formed the New Party which eventually became the British Union of Fascists.

At the height of the depression nearly three million insured workers were without jobs, not including the self-employed, agricultural workers and women who either did not, or were not, eligible for registration. In the south-east, one worker in nine was on the dole. In Tyneside, Lancashire, South Wales and Clydeside, where a reliance of work had rested with the traditional industries, unemployment was at one in three or four of the workforce. In Bishop Auckland there had been 33 pits employing 28,000 miners. By 1935 only thirteen pits were still in production with a total workforce of 6,500 men employed on a part-time basis. In 1934, 67.8 per cent of insured workers in Jarrow were on the dole. In Gateshead the figure was 44.23 per cent and in Merthyr it was 61.9 per cent. The coal industry, in particular, had failed to recapture its export markets of the years before the Great War and was also facing intense competition at home from gas and electricity. Yet despite the slump, significant improvements in productivity were registered, especially in the large modern pits sunk in Nottinghamshire, Yorkshire and Scotland. By 1939 coal-cutting equipment was in use on the majority of faces and 61 per cent of coal was cut by machine. The Coal Mines Act of 1930 also set production quotas for each district and determined a minimum price. Further Government attempts at reorganisation were resisted by the coal-owners, but in 1939 the royalties of the mining companies were nationalised and the task of reorganising the industry was handed over to the Coal Commission.

It was in an attempt to publicise their plight that the National Unemployed Workers Movement (NUWM) organised a series of marches and demonstrations throughout the country. On 1st October 1931, several hundred demonstrators gathered in the square in front of Salford Town Hall to protest at cuts in unemployment benefit. In a pitched battle with police, twelve demonstrators were arrested. A week later, 5,000 men assembled at Ardwick Green, their intention being to walk to Manchester Town Hall and present a petition. When the police informed them that their intended route into the city was considered 'provocative' fighting broke out. The following day Manchester was witnessing scenes reminiscent of the General Strike, with police mounting guard on public buildings, and the mobilisation of Special Constables occuring on an unprecedented scale. The NUWM continued its campaign into 1932, the worst disturbances occurring in Belfast where the police were forced to open fire on demonstrators in self defence.

Due to economy cuts, between 1931-35 an unemployed man with a wife and three children to support could expect to receive 29/3d a week benefit or as 'transitional payments' once benefit had been exhaustsed. Transitional payments were subject to means testing, a particularly vicious piece of legislation in which the earnings, savings, pensions and other assets of a family were taken into account before an award was made. It was automatically assumed that the assets of a family were available to support an unemployed man. Children, if in work and if they lived at home, were expected to support out of work parents. Neighbours were positively encouraged to spy and inform on one another. Large numbers were cut off from benefit by the means test. In Lancashire, it has been claimed that a third of all applicants were refused help.

It was not until Sir Malcolm Stewart's ideas were accepted in the Special Areas (Amendment) Act, 1937, that the possibilities for creating any large-scale employment occured. Sir Malcolm's proposal was that, in return for opening a factory in a depressed area, a firm should be offered tax, rent and rates incentives for a period of five years. Sir Malcolm's vision led to the opening of a number of trading estates, where firms could lease premises with all services laid on. Initially, the trading estates attracted only light industries, but by the end of 1937 unemployment figures for the Special Areas had fallen by 155,000, though 67,000 of these were due to people moving to other areas in search of work. By 1937, rearmament was beginning to take up industrial spare capacity and slowly but surely new jobs were being created.

The Rise of Germany

In Germany in 1932, unemployment stood at six million and was still rising. It was out of the misery of unemployment and low pay for those fortunate enough to be in work, that the class, ideological, and racial doctrines of the National Socialist Party (Nazis) grew and prospered in the Weimar Republic. In July 1932, the Nazis polled 37.3 per cent in the general election. Under the republic's system of proportional representation, this poll gave the Nazis 230 seats in the Reichstag, making them the largest single party in parliament. Despite his known dislike of the Nazis and their politics, aging President Hindenburg had little alternative but to summon the Nazi leader Adolf Hitler to the Chancellorship. It was January 1933.

Adolf Hitler was without doubt a charismatic figure; he was also a political opportunist. He was, however, totally committed

27 August 1938. A queue nearly a mile long formed in Camden High Street outside one of the St Pancras depots, where people were to receive and be fitted for their gas masks.

in his desire to see Germany once more established as the leading European power.

Hitler's first priority was to make his own position and authority unassailable. On 28th February, a decree was issued under Article 48 of the Constitution suspending normal civil liberties. In March came the 'Communist' plot culminating in the burning down of the Reichstag. Using Article 48, Hitler expelled the 83 Communist members of parliament, and by reaching an accord with the Centre Party achieved the majority required to pass the Enabling Law. The Enabling Law allowed the Chancellor to issue legislation without having to seek the consent of parliament.

From 1934 onwards, Hitler was to push rearmament and the reinflation of the German economy to the limit. It was not a straightforward task. Germany lacked foreign exchange which hampered the supply of imports, especially Swedish iron ore, and the only raw material that she possessed in relative abundance was coal.

On 9th March 1935, Germany formally acknowledged for the first time that she possessed an Air Force (*Luftwaffe*). A week later, conscription was introduced, the peace-time strength of the Army being raised to 550,000 men. By the end of the year the German Navy had launched no less than nineteen submarines, though these were coastal craft more suitable for training than for actual offensive operations.

In 1936 Hitler, playing the political opportunist, ordered German troops into the demilitarised Rhineland. Britain and France failed to act and Hitler gained the diplomatic initiative.

The Anschluss & Czechoslovakia

Hitler had long dreamed of one day incorporating his native Austria into the Reich and by the beginning of 1938 he was ready to make his move.

On 12th February 1938, Austrian Chancellor Kurt von Schuschnigg visited Hitler at Berchtesgaden. With typical Nazi panache, the route was lined somewhat menacingly with troops from Germany's 120,000 — strong Austrian Legion. By the end of the meeting, Schuschnigg had agreed to include Austrian Nazis in his Cabinet. The question of unification (Anschluss) was raised but no formal agreement was reached. Hitler got the shock of his life a couple of weeks later when Schuschnigg announced that the question of unification would have to be decided by the people of Austria by plebiscite. Fearing that the

23 August 1938 and ARP gas mask drill is available to swimmers at the Empire Pool, Wembley.

vote could go against unification, the German High Command were ordered to improvise an invasion plan during the night of 9th/10th March. German troops crossed the Austrian frontier on the 11th and the country was annexed the following day.

On the 13th, Adolf Hitler drove in triumph through the streets of Vienna. Once again Britain and France dithered and did nothing.

Neville Chamberlain's idea of purchasing peace through appeasement was that any settlement should involve concessions on both sides, which would be honoured in perpetuity. Czechoslovakia was another matter.

On 20th February 1938, Hitler gave a speech in which he promised protection for all Germans living outside the Reich. The speech was seized upon by the Sudeten Nazis in Czechoslovakia to intensify their demands for self-determination

On 28th/29th April, the first of a series of Anglo-French meetings took place to consider the implications of German intentions towards Czechoslovakia. British policy towards the Czechs was both ill-informed and unsympathetic. Czechoslovakia was not seen as a bastion of democracy to be defended by a "last chance for Anglo-German understanding". The French on the other hand, were bound by treaty to aid the Czechs if they were attacked. However, the French feared that in the event of war they would be without British support. Outwardly the Anglo-French conversations were shown as the working out of a joint policy. Behind the scenes both governments had decided to abandon the Czechs to their fate, but a public announcement to that fact would have been political suicide. At all costs the Czechs had to be deserted but at the same time French honour had to be seen to be preserved.

During May the Sudeten Nazi leader Konrad Henlein visited London. Henlein reported back to Berlin that the British Government was sympathetic to the Sudeten cause. In any case Chamberlain saw no benefit to Great Britain in an independent Czechoslovakia. Indeed, he shared with Hitler the dislike of the Czech alliances with France and the Soviet Union, though he was also influenced by the fact that the Dominions had little sympathy for a British guarantee.

On 20th May, two days before the Czech Municipal Elections, Hitler ordered General Keital to dust off the plans for a pre-emptive strike against the Czechs whilst holding a defensive line in the west just in case the French decided to intervene. Hitler believed that military action against the Czechs had to take place quickly so that Britain and France would not have time to react. Within days, Europe was gripped with the news that German troops were massing along the Czech frontier.

With 35 divisions, and tanks far superior to anything the Germans had, the Czech Army would certainly have given a good account of itself in a shooting war. The German Army, however, had expanded so rapidly that many units were untrained. There was a serious shortage of officers, only six weeks supply of munitions, and fuel reserves stood at only 25 per cent of the mobilisation requirement. In the air, the *Luftwaffe* was in the middle of a transition phase caused by new generations of fighters and bombers which had been introduced from 1936 onwards. They were suffering from a high accident rate, and on 1st August 1938 *Luftwaffe* operational strength for aircraft stood at 49 per cent of the bomber force and 70 per cent for the fighter arm. The whole of the *Luftwaffe* was only 57 per cent operational, and only with drastic reductions in flying hours and training schedules could the force be brought up to a respectable in-commission rate, but that would still take at least eight weeks to achieve. To add to the *Luftwaffe's* problems, the reserves of some aircraft lubricants stood at only

six per cent of the mobilisation requirement. The *Luftwaffe* was in no fit state to get involved in a war of attrition.

The German ace was her propaganda machine. Throughout the summer, a superbly conducted campaign gave the impression that Germany's military capability was far greater than it actually was. Visiting dignitaries were taken from one airfield to another and shown the might of the *Luftwaffe*. What they weren't privy to was the fact that some of the squadrons of modern aircraft were flying from one field to another just in front of the visitors. The Czechs would not act without the promise of help from either Russia, Britain or France.

On 4th September, the Czech Government finally cracked. Fearing civil war, President Benes agreed to all Sudeten demands. On the 13th, Hitler demanded self-determination for the Sudetenland. The following day rioting broke out and Martial Law was declared. Henlein fled to Berlin. British attempts at deterring the Germans consisted of diplomatic moves pointing to the probability of intervention, while at the same time positively discouraging the Czechs from fighting by hinting at the improbability of British intervention. Hitler then demanded the annexation of the Sudetenland and the situation became potentially explosive. Chamberlain offered to go to see Hitler in one last effort to secure a peaceful solution.

28 September 1938. The call goes out for women to join the Auxiliary Territorial Service, the object of which was to relieve troops from non-combatant duties. By the end of 1939 there were 43,000 girls serving in the women's auxiliary services which included the Women's Auxiliary Air Force (WAAFs), the Women's Royal Naval Service (Wrens) and the Auxiliary Territorial Service (ATS). The photograph was taken at Bloomsbury.

The French panicked and abdicated all initiatives to Britain, President Daladier begging Chamberlain to do something — anything to avoid France having to honour her treaty obligations. Chamberlain flew to Berchtesgaden.

During their three hour talk, Hitler made it quite plain to Chamberlain that unless Britain accepted Germany's claims there was little point in continuing the converstation. Chamberlain was in no position to negotiate an on the spot agreement, however he offered to consult his Cabinet if Germany, in the meantime, would refrain from opening hostilities. Hitler agreed. Chamberlain was convinced that only the cession of the Sudetenland would halt a German invasion. Three days later Daladier came to London and agreed a plan whereby Germany would receive all areas in Czechoslovakia containing a majority German population. The Czechs found the proposals unacceptable but were left in no doubt whatsoever that Britain would not fight and that France would ignore her treaty obligations.

On the 22nd, Chamberlain met Hitler at Godesberg. Sensing victory, Hitler upped the price of peace. He insisted that Czech forces evacuate the German areas but that they must leave the military installations intact. He also demanded a plebiscite to be held in all other areas of Czechoslovakia which had a German minority. Chamberlain was well aware that British public opinion was hardening against further concessions, and on his return to London he held a series of crisis meetings with the Cabinet and later the French.

Lord Halifax urged Chamberlain to make one last effort to reach an agreement with Hitler. The outcome was that Sir Horace Wilson was to deliver to Hitler a personal letter appealing to him to allow the details of any settlement to be overseen by an international committee of Czech, German and British officials. If Hitler refused, Wilson was to tell him that France would stand by the Czechs and Britain would stand by France. In Britain, air raid trenches were dug in public parks and what few anti-aircraft guns there were, were sited around London.

On the morning of the 26th, British and French officials discussed the military implications of the crisis and war was considered to be a viable option. Later, Chamberlain informed his Cabinet that Britain would support France in the event of war. Hitler had lost his chance for a pre-emptive attack. A conference was hurriedly arranged.

On 29th September, the Munich Conference was convened. Neither Czechoslovakia nor the Soviet Union were represented. In reality the conference was little more than a ceremony, though Hitler was persuaded to agree to a progressive occupation of the Sudetenland, and a commission to determine the status of the remaining areas with predominantly German populations to be occupied by German troops.

On the morning of the 30th Chamberlain and Hitler signed — upon the initiative of the former — a declaration that the two countries would in future settle any sources of difference by negotiation.

The result of Munich was that Hitler had gained everything he had wanted and at the same time had destroyed France's military credibility. Also, he had successfully isolated Soviet Russia and Poland, and inflicted a diplomatic defeat upon Great

December 1938. This former air raid trench on Clapham Common takes on a more permanent form having been roofed over and lined with concrete.

April 1939. An Islington tobaconist announces the good news that the increase in tobacco duty has not been passed on to the customer — yet.

Britain.

Chamberlain had, however, averted war. He came home to an albeit short hero's welcome. The British press applauded him but at the same time voiced concern over the future. Peace had been sacrificed for a semblance of peace.

Poland

On 24th March 1939, Britain and France agreed to resist any German aggression against Belgium, Holland and Switzerland. A week later, Britain said that she would stand by France in guaranteeing Poland's frontiers. On the 3rd and 11th April, Hitler issued orders for the Wehrmacht to prepare for the invasion of Poland.

With a population of 27 million, Poland's affairs were dominated by her relations with her neighbours, none of whom were too pleased with the frontiers settled upon her by the Treaty of Versailles. By the end of 1921, the infant Polish Republic had fought no less than six wars and had heavily defeated the Russians at Komarow. But Poland was bitter. She had been left to fight the Soviet Union alone despite the existence of mutual aid treaties with Britain and France.

On 25th January 1932, Poland signed a treaty of non-aggression with Russia, and on 26th January 1934, concluded a similar pact with Nazi Germany.

The real threat to Poland came after the Nazi Party had gained control of the Free City of Danzig. There is plenty of evidence that the Poles had seriously considered launching an all-out preventive war against Germany but had refrained from

doing so because Britain and France had refused to get involved. Hitler, inspired by the apparent inability of the Western powers to get their act together and do anything to stop him, decided that the time had come to settle Danzig's future. To Hitler, Danzig's future lay in her incorporation into the Reich. The German leader demanded the return of Danzig and access to the city across Polish territory. In return, he offered the Poles a guarantee of their frontiers. Poland rejected the demands out of hand.

On 20th August, the world was stunned by the news that the Soviet Union and Nazi Germany had signed a trade agreement. The same day, Hitler once again demanded the annexation of Danzig. Three days later, Russia and Germany signed a non-aggression pact undertaking not to attack each other. They also concluded a secret agreement to divide Poland and the Baltic States between them.

On 24th August, Britain requested American help in the growing Polish crisis. United States Ambassador Kennedy's near hysterical reporting of the situation gave the impression in Washington that Chamberlain was attempting to force the Poles into unilateral concessions with Germany. In fact, what Chamberlain wanted was that the Poles state their willingness to negotiate in order to put Hitler in the wrong should he attack. Also, if Hitler agreed to negotiate, then with a little luck, the Poles would be able to drag out the talks until the winter rains made invasion impossible.

Dawn on the 26th had been the time set by Hitler for the invasion of Poland to commence, but on the evening of the 25th, Mussolini informed him that Italy was in no fit state to

Fun down on the farm during that long hot summer of 1939.

Their Royal Highnesses The Duke and Duchess of Kent review the London Fire Brigade (LFB) and Auxiliary Fire Service (AFS) in Hyde Park. June 1939.

get involved in a general war without massive military aid. The plans were cancelled. On the 25th, Hitler had met with Sir Neville Henderson, our ambassador to Berlin. Henderson was told that Germany desired a settlement with Britain and that he, Hitler, was prepared to guarantee the British Empire and would approach London with an 'offer' once the Polish question had been settled. On the evening of the 29th, Hitler announced his willingness to negotiate providing a Polish emissary arrived in Berlin by noon the following day. He denied that this was in effect an ultimatum, though he still hoped to divide London and Warsaw. He was convinced that Chamberlain could be tempted into an alliance with Germany, and that two interesting possibilities would then arise.

Firstly, the Poles might refuse to talk in which case the British would be justified in revoking their treaty obligations. Secondly, if a Polish emissary did arrive and talks broke down, then Chamberlain might refuse to fight on the grounds that the Poles had provoked war. Chamberlain to his credit had no intention of being drawn into such a trap and informed his Cabinet that the demand for a Polish emissary was unacceptable and that any Anglo-German agreement depended upon a just settlement for Poland backed by an international guarantee.

At 4pm on the 31st, Hitler decided that he could wait no longer and ordered the invasion of Poland to take place at dawn the follwing day.

At dawn on 1st September, the German Battleship *Schleswig-Holstein,* moored in the port of Danzig on a friendship visit, opened fire at close-range on the Polish fortifications at Westerplatte. An hour later, German armour crossed the Polish frontier, the first serious fighting occurring in and around Gross-Klonia. The *Luftwaffe* launched a series of air strikes against Warsaw and other cities, and were challenged by the Polish Air Force (PAF). With less than two hundred fighter planes, the PAF was forced to resort to head-on attacks that unnerved many of the *Luftwaffe* pilots making them break formation and dump their bombs away from their intended targets. Obliged to engage the *Luftwaffe* wherever and whenever possible, the PAF's combat strength was whittled away.

The Polish Army was overwhelmed in many sectors as it was deployed to meet political rather than tactical strategies.

At this late stage, said that they were still willing to negotiate if German troops were withdrawn. Hitler, anticipating a short, sharp war of no more than two weeks, rejected the proposal. That afternoon the War Office issued instructions to the Regular Army and all Territorial Army units that general mobilisation had been proclaimed and that all troops should report to their depots. Under the Defence Regulations, the 'blackout' came into force at sunset and would last for 2,061 consecutive nights. On the first night, however, Coventry was totally blacked out except for the traffic lights which someone forgot to switch off!

A Lufthansa Junkers Ju52 tri-motor at Croydon Airport on 27 August 1939. This type of aircraft was to see extensive wartime service with the *Luftwaffe* as a transport and troop carrier. This particular machine has been named after that immortal German World War One fighter ace Oswald Boelcke.

Boys from Dulwich College at Cranbrook, Kent, following their evacuation at the height of the Czech Crisis.

28 August 1939. Evacuation rehearsals begin. Three brothers and their sister arrive at Friar's Street School in south east London.

An identification label round their necks, a gas mask in a cardboard box and a few personal belongings. Evacuation rehearsal at Friar's Street School.

The adventure begins. Parents, relatives and friends wave goodbye at Blackhorse Road Station. Most left by either train or bus but parties from the east London suburb of Dagenham were evacuated to East Anglia by boat.

A trolleybus hisses to a halt and a policeman hurries along children from Benwell Road School, Holloway.

Tears at Kings Cross Station from little Freddie Soper of Winston Street School.

Students act as stretcher bearers as patients are evacuated from Guy's Hospital in Green Line buses.

Left. A familiar scene throughout London. The well-conceived evacuation by rail was the brainchild of London Passenger Transport Board (LPTB) vice chairman Frank Pick. His scheme kept the vast majority of children away from the busy mainline terminal stations by using the Underground and buses to ferry them out to suburban stations to join their trains.

Liverpool Street Station, 1 September 1939. After the morning rush hour only skeleton suburban services operated so as to clear the tracks for evacuation specials.

Mothers and children from the Streatham area walk to their local railway station.

Waiting for a train at Streatham. Over at Ealing Broadway the Great Western Railway ran fifty-eight evacuation trains which departed at nine minute intervals and carried a total of just over 44,000 people.

September 1939

On 1st September, the evacuation of children, toddlers, expectant mothers, the disabled and some hospital patients began in earnest from London and other towns and cities considered to be potential targets for enemy bombers.

Despite a wealth of official publicity during that long hot summer of 1939, the numbers of children registered for evacuation fell far short of Government expectations. Of the 73,000 Birmingham children entitled to be evacuated, less than a third presented themselves on the day. Only eight per cent of children were evacuated from Rotherham and only fifteen per cent from Sheffield, and of 23,000 Nottingham children, less than 5,000 went. In London less than fifty per cent of the children left, so that when the Blitz began there were at least 500,000 youngsters living in the metropolitan area.

However, in three days nearly one and a half million were evacuated without a single accident or casualty. London's evacuation scheme centred on the railway system and was based on plans drawn up during the Munich Crisis of 1938. By using the London Underground and buses, evacuees were kept away from the capital's mainline terminals, being taken instead to suburban stations such as New Barnet, Ealing Broadway, Stratford, Watford and Wimbledon, where special trains left at regular intervals for the reception areas. There was little choosing in the destination and though school groups did keep together, trains were simply filled to capacity and sent on their way.

On Saturday 2nd September, despite general mobilisation having been proclaimed the previous afternoon and the continuation of the evacuation programme, some semblance of normality was maintained. Around 370,000 fans travelled to watch League football games despite travelling difficulties.

Spurs arrived at West Bromwich Albion with only minutes to spare before the kick-off but managed to score twice early on in the game. Cecil Shaw, Albion's left back, walked off dejectedly at full time having missed a penalty. As he walked down the player's tunnel he was told that his wife was about to give birth and it is said that he smiled for the first time all afternoon. At Blackpool there was an incident when a whisky bottle was thrown at the Wolves goalkeeper. Order was restored when the referee asked for two policemen to patrol inside the ground! Many amateur football matches were cancelled through players being called up for ARP duties and stewards at the Jockery Club announced that they would meet within the next few days to make a decision regarding the future of horse racing should war be declared.

The international situation was still deteriorating. The *Wehrmacht* were pushing into Polish territory, overwhelming many sectors before the defenders could call in reinforcement. Norway, Sweden, Denmark, Finland, Iceland, Latvia and Estonia declared their neutrality, and Italy and Japan both declared their intentions not to take part.

When Prime Minister Neville Chamberlain came to the despatch box in the House of Commons at 7.30pm, he must have felt a lonely man indeed. He was virtually isolated, his supporters falling away on all sides. He had made desperate efforts to secure a lasting peace with Germany and even at this late stage he told the House that a conference could be convened if Hitler would withdraw his troops. It was not the news that the majority of members wished to hear; appeasement was no longer a diplomacy that satisfied public opinion — it had failed. Chamberlain sat down before a silent house, no cheers, no applause, nothing. The acting Labour leader Arthur Greenwood rose to his feet to respond.

Encouraged by members of all parties he spoke. "Every minute's delay now means the loss of life, imperilling our national interests . . . imperilling the foundations of our national honours." The House broke up in confusion.

The ministers Hore-Belisha, Anderson, de la Warr, Colville, Dorman-Smith, Stanley, Wallace and Elliot, met with Sir John Simon. Later, Sir John and a group of his 'mutineers' went to see the Prime Minister and told him bluntly that the Cabinet would no longer co-operate with him until war was declared. At last, Chamberlain spoke, "Right, gentlemen, this means war." At 11pm the Cabinet met in an emergency session.

At 9am on Sunday 3 September, an ultimatum was delivered to Berlin. Two hours later it expired without reply. At 11.15 am the Prime Minister spoke to the nation on the radio. No assurance had been received "Consequently this country is now at war with Germany."

To many, the policy of appeasement is seen as something unique to Neville Chamberlain. This is not so as he was following a pattern in our foreign policy going back seventy-five years which was in a way the only course open to a nation both economically stretched and trying to defend a far flung empire. The difference was the Chamberlain's predecessors had not come up against a political opponent as aggressive, as opportunist or as fanatical as Adolf Hitler.

Sunday 3 September 1939. Troops arriving in the city "read all about it." Military reservists and Air Raid Precautions (ARP) personnel had either been called up or placed on alert on 24 August. It was not until the afternoon of 2 September that the War Office issued instructions to regular and territorial units that general mobilization had been proclaimed and that all troops should report back to their depots as soon as possible. By the time the soldiers in this photograph were reading their newspaper, the first battle of the war had already taken place. At 11.27am, the air raid sirens sounded their onimous warning over London. A few minutes later the all clear was given, it had been a false alarm caused by a single French aircraft. However, in those few, short minutes, two groups of RAF fighters had been scrambled into the air over the Thames, and when they engaged one another in combat in what later became known as the Battle of Barking Creek, two planes were shot down and a pilot was killed.

17

Civil Defence

At the height of the bombing approximately 1½ million people in Britain were involved in Air Raid Precaution (ARP) work of which about 80 per cent were part-time volunteers and nearly 25 per cent were women.

The wardens job was essentially in two separate parts. He had to judge the extent and type of damage in his area so the Control Centre could send the appropriate rescue services. His local knowledge was vital if time and effort were to be saved hunting for survivors trapped beneath debris. Secondly, he was responsible for getting the 'bombed-out' to some sort of shelter or a Rest Centre. Over 90 per cent of wardens were part-timers and one in six was a woman.

First Aid Posts (FAP) were usually manned by a doctor, a trained nurse and nursing auxiliaries. There was normally one FAP to every 15,000 people though larger towns and cities were also equipped with mobile units which could be called in to reinforce a hard pressed fixed post or even a hospital.

Under the direct orders of a Control Centre were the First Aid Parties. Each party consisted of four men and a driver. All were experienced first aid workers having been trained by either the Red Cross, St John's Ambulance, or the St Andrew's Society. Their main task was to help the Rescue Men release trapped casualties and then administer what aid they could before deciding whether or not a casualty needed further treatment at a FAP or hospital.

The task of the Rescue Men was the really backbreaking work in Civil Defence. Often amid fire and with the ever present danger of explosion from fractured gas pipes these men searched the debris for both victims and survivors.

The London Fire Brigade was without doubt the best equipped and trained firefighting force in the country. Equipment was constantly being updated and drills soon incorporated the latest techniques. However for all its skill and dedication the LFB on its own would have been hard pressed to deal with the emregencies arising out of an air raid.

In March 1938 the first volunteers for the Auxiliary Fire Service (AFS) enrolled in London and though recruiting was initially low, numbers gradually increased and the first AFS stations were commissioned the following September at Bunhill Row, Moreland Street and Gravel Lane. The training of AFS crews was carried out by regular LFB officers.

AFS equipment usually consisted of trailer pumps designed for towing behind any suitable vehicles. These trailer pumps of which there were four types, had a pumping capability of between 120gpm and 900gpm and were manufactured by a number of companies including Coventry-Climas, Dennis, Scammel and Worthington-Simpson. All of these types were on two wheels with pumps powered by four-cylinder petrol engines. There was also a four-wheeled pump supplied by both Sulzer and Tangye and these were powered by Ford V8 engines. There were two basic AFS self-contained engines. Most of these were based upon a Fordson or Leyland chassis with a Sulzer pump able to deliver 900gpm. The second type, known as an 'extra heavy unit' was again based upon the Ford/Leyland chassis but equipped with a pump capable of delivering 1,400 gpm through six jets. All the emergency units were painted battleship grey and lacked the brass and chrome adornments of regular machines.

On the 30th August 1939, all AFS and regular units were issued with steel helmets and respirators and the Home Office announced that the weekly rates of pay for full-time AFS crews would be £3 for men, £2 for women, 25/- for youths aged 17-18, and £1 for youths aged 16-17.

As the bombing continued into 1941, the groundswell of opinion in the fire service favouring a nationalised force grew. The attitude of local authorities to the fire service was amazingly varied, from totally apathetic to excellent. In some towns the local authorities had still not provided a towing vehicle for each trailer pump, and it was not uncommon to see firemen having to manhandle pumps to blitz fires. On the evening of the 18th April 1941, Home Secretary Herbert Morrison met with Sir George Gater, secretary to the Minister of Home Security, Sir Arthur Dixon, head of the fire service division of the Home Office, and Commander Firebrace of the London Fire Brigade. Within four hours the principles of a National Fire Service were laid down and on the 22nd May, the Bill received the royal assent.

The broad plan was to amalgamate the 1,400 existing brigades in the United Kingdom into twelve regions, each being further sub-divided into fire forces. The government was to undertake the whole cost of the emergency element of the service and to pay 25 per cent towards the normal annual costs of the regular brigade.

Artist's impression of an underground air raid shelter intended for suburbia. However, it was the Anderson shelter which became a familiar sight at the bottom of most gardens and many examples survive to this day (1989). The shelter was named after Sir John Anderson, Secretary of State for Home Affairs. It was cheap to produce and easy to erect.

" 'Ullo, 'ullo, 'ullo, what's all this then eh?'' It's the 5 September 1939 and the peculiar structure attracting attention from this passing policeman is not a bird table. It is in fact one of a number of boards coated with gas sensitive paint which were placed at strategic points around the city.

"Oh I do like to be beside the seaside." The holiday atmosphere of this photograph taken at West End Green, Hampstead, on 5 September 1939 belies the serious intentions of its' subjects. Anyone who could spare an hour or so was invited to come along and fill sandbags that were desperately needed elsewhere in London.

ARP spotter on the roof of the Grosvenor House Hotel, September 1939.

ARP wardens run to give the alarm during a daylight air raid exercise in
Chelsea.

Lambeth Headquarters of the London Fire Brigade (LFB) was where learner drivers received their training.
Many Auxiliary Fire Service (AFS) drivers had never passed a driving test and because fire appliances were
exempt from the 20mph speed limit it was considered expedient to give them thorough training.

Divide six jam tarts by nine children. Alternatively just where do you put your Anderson shelter when you haven't a garden? Neighbours John Storey and JG Lawrence resolved the latter problem by erecting their Andersons indoors — Mr Storey in his sitting room and Mr Lawrence in his kitchen. Andersons consisted of two corrugated steel walls which met in a ridge at the top and were bolted to sturdy rails to give the structure strength. The shelter was then "planted" three feet into the ground and covered with at least eighteen inches of earth. The entrance was protected by a steel shield and a blast wall made of soil. Approximately 2,250,000 Andersons were distributed free of charge, but in October 1939 a change in Government policy meant that any person earning over £5 a week had to buy their own at prices ranging from £6.14s to £10.18s each. In our photograph Mrs Storey has popped in to the Lawrences for a cuppa — but who will get the jam tarts?

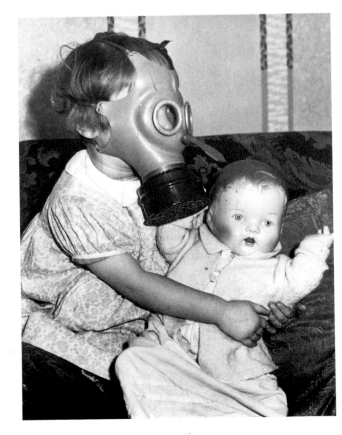

19 October 1938. This young lady wears one of the very latest issue of gas masks designed for toddlers. Many youngsters found the wearing of respirators a frightening experience, and an attempt was made to allieviate some of their worries by manufacturing new models in bright colours of red rubber and blue enamel. Toddlers' respirators differed from those supplied to adults in that breath was expelled through a valve in the nose piece.

Solving a blackout problem on the railway in October 1939. Shunting was a tricky enough operation at any time let alone in the blackout. To make shunting locomotives as visible as possible to those on the ground, the buffer beams were painted white and the lights dimmed.

Black-Out
Tomorrow: 4.35 p.m.

SUMMER-TIME ends at 3 a.m. tomorrow, and from next week the black-out will descend on Britain an hour earlier. The clock goes BACK.

Many offices and warehouses are planning to close earlier, but, even so, workers will have to go home in the black-out.

The departure of B.S.T. is regretted by shopkeepers and business men, but farmers and others who have to start work early in the day welcome the return of G.M.T. Shopkeepers deplore the change (see Page Nine).

Make note of the revised black-out times :

Tonight   5.36*—6.55a.m.†
Tomorrow 4.35†—6.57 a.m.†

    * Summer Time
    † Winter Time

South London based artist Albert Perry at work with some of his pupils during his daily gas mask drill in August 1941. A gas attack against our civilian population was, thankfully, one horror not perpetrated and there is no proof that such an attack was ever considered. But gas had been used with devastating effect by both sides during the Great War and more recently by the Italians in Abyssinia.

Left: "Gas, gas, gas, gas, gas!" February 1940. During the period now known as the Phoney War, the lack of enemy bombing raids against our cities led to a blasé approach to ARP. Gas masks were left at home and full-time ARP workers were often accused of sponging their wages, the outcome of which was that many were laid off. This photograph was issued to serve as a reminder of just why wardens carried rattles.

8 April 1941. Testing the effectiveness of gas masks. Girls from a city office queue up to pass through a gas chamber.

June 1941. A suprise gas test in Kingston was given an authentic flavour by the letting off of tear gas grenades.

Gas test in Holborn. Bobbies observe the top of a pillarbox coated with gas sensitive paint.

Publicity photograph taken in October 1940 of some of the first shelter
"season ticket" holders.

City girls snatch forty winks during London's third alert of the day.

Pupils at the Hugh Myddleton School, Clerkenwell, get down to some serious card playing and Beano reading during an alert.

Tea up! One of London's eight Tube shelters which were due to be operational by the end of 1942. These shelters were the largest in the UK and had a combined capacity for 68,000 people. Each was fitted out with wire-mesh bunks, snack bars and sick bays. This particular shelter situated in South London, had sixteen sections which were named after famous British admirals such as Anson, Beatty, Evans and Jellicoe. The mesh bunks can be seen in the centre background of the photograph.

A windometre installed at a wardens' post at Hill Top, Hampstead. It was designed by warden Mr K McKillop and was to be used for plotting wind direction in the event of a gas attack.

Hackney ARP wardens managed to acquire an assortment of obsolete weapons for drill purposes. The wardens quite rightly believed that at Church parades and during long marches there was nothing like carrying a rifle to smarten up the proceedings. The rifles include Martin Henry's and muzzle loaders, the drill masters looks to have had an accident at some time

War Weapons Week, May 1941. Chiswick and Brentford civil defence workers present *Why Wardens Wear Ws*. The sketch was written by George Greig (on the right) and all the words of the dialogue began with the letter W.

The City of London Police give their first performance since their rehearsal room was bombed. In order to fulfil its engagement the band had to buy, beg or borrow new instruments.

War Weapons Week May 1941. LFB fireboats give a lunch hour display. One of the LFBs most famous fireboats was the *Massey Shaw,* which built in 1935 and with a top speed of around 12 knots in calm weather, took part in the Dunkirk evacuations. The *Massey Shaw* made three return trips as well as ferrying troops from the beaches to transports standing farther out. On her way back to London she was slowly overhauled by the French naval auxiliary *Emile de Champ* off Margate. The Frenchman was about two hundred yards abeam when it struck a mine and sank within minutes. The fireboat altered course, picked up about thirty badly injured survivors and took them to Ramsgate. Of the *Massey Shaw's* crew, Sub Officer AJ May was awarded the DSM and firemen EG Wright and HA Wray were mentioned in dispatches.

Spot the dog is one of the crew of this three-wheeled *Derby* appliance stationed at West Croydon in April 1941.

Can you see me mother? Smiles for the camera from London AFS crews at Hyde Park in 1941 where they had been inspected by the Lord Privy Seal, the Rt Hon Clement Attlee.

What must have been one of the most unusual fire brigades in the country was the London Zoo firefighting unit where even the animals were pressed into service. The unit was photographed during a pracitice drill. The notice about feeding times has nothing to do with the unit.

NEW LIVES - NEW NEEDS

CINEMA USHER becomes A.F.S. HERO

(braver than any film one)

Last year you saw him marshalling the film queues — tall, white-gloved, immaculate. Now the gloves are off all right! He's in the A.F.S., and night after night he answers the call of danger. What an abrupt, dramatic change — and what a tremendous toll it has taken of his nerves and stamina.

Girls of the Wood Green AFS station start up a trailer pump for wet drill. It was during the war that the trailer pump came into its own as an invaluable piece of equipment designed for towing behind any suitable vehicle. Their main advantage was that they could often be manhandled over debris and around bomb craters. There were numerous types ranging in pumping capacity from 100 to 900 gpm and powered by anything ranging from JAP motorcycle engines to Ford V8s. The most powerful trailer pumps were four wheeled versions built by either Sulzer or Tangye but these had to be towed by regular LFB vehicles.

"This little piggy went to market." These men at an AFS station in South West London were really into the self sufficiency way of life.

17 September 1941. Toys made by members of the AFS went on display at Old Ford
prior to being distributed to child welfare centres.

13 July 1942 and volunteers for the firefighting unit at NAAFI headquarters, London, run
out their trailer pump.

Practising putting out fires with a stirrup pump.

All Will Be Trained to Fire Guard

COMPULSORY training for fire guards was announced by Miss Ellen Wilkinson, Parliamentary Secretary to the Ministry of Home Security, in a speech at Newcastle yesterday.

The scheme will apply to fire guards serving under the local authority and also to those at business and Government premises.

But the training will not be an extra liability, Miss Wilkinson pointed out. It will take place during the 48 hours of part-time service a month.

The recent "Baedeker" raids, said Miss Wilkinson, had shown very clearly how vital a part fire guards could play when an incendiary attack was made on a town.

"The National Fire Service," she went on, "naturally concentrate on the big fires that break out, and it then depends on the fire guards alone whether other serious fires start or whether this is prevented."

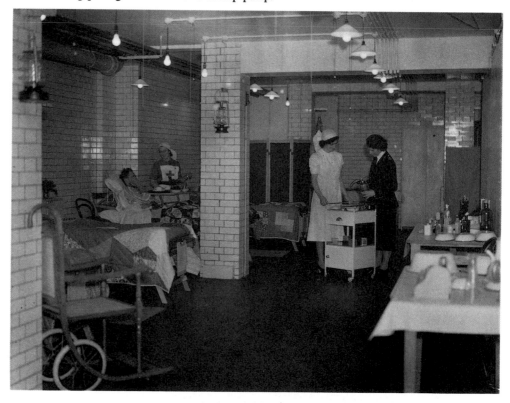

The capital's only underground hospital in 1941 was situated below Cheapside. There were only two wards, one for men and one for women, each containing six beds. The patchwork quilts were a gift from Canada.

Bethnal Green ARP Rescue Squad practice making and using a temporary suspension bridge.

The Imperial War Museum Firefighting School. There were twelve Ministry of Works & Buildings schools, two of which were in London, for training civil servants in firefighting. The photograph shows pupils learning how to tie a chair knot which was used for rescue purposes. The girl on the left has a completed chair knot in position under her arms, the others are battling on.

Training in tunnelling. This method of rescue was used where the removal of debris would either take too long or could cause a collapse of debris onto the casualties.

LCC heavy rescue unit on a tunnelling exercise using breathing apparatus.

This is no drill. A rescue man burrows towards an elderly lady trapped by debris during a daylight raid in February 1941.

The Home Front

On 27th September 1939, Sir John Simon introduced the Emergency War Budget. The first commodity to be rationed was petrol. An increase in whisky duty was expected to bring in £3,500,000 in a full year. The basic duty on tobacco was increased from 11s6d to 13s6d per pound, adding 1½d per ounce to the price in the shops. Sugar duty was also increased which led to higher prices in the shops of tinned fruit, jam, marmalade, syrup and sweetened milk.

The rationing of basic foodstuffs was introduced in January 1940. The weekly allowance per person included 2ozs tea (non for the under fives), 2ozs butter, 4ozs margarine, 4ozs sugar, 2ozs sweets and 2ozs fats. Extra cheese was allowed to those workers who had no canteen facilities, and a special ration was available to vegetarians who undertook to surrender their meat coupons. WS Morrison, the then Minister of Food, also announced the rationing of meats. The intended ration was to be 6ozs per head per day, though this was limited to prime cuts only. People would still be free to buy cheaper cuts of meat to the cash value of 6ozs of prime beef, mutton or pork.

April 1940 saw the annual Budget. Sir John spoke in the House of Commons for two hours and seven minutes. In that time, he revealed that he estimated expenditure for the coming year at £2,667,000,000 of which he expected to raise £1,234,000,000 from revenue. The 1940 Budget, when it was announced, was to that date the largest sum ever raised in one year's taxation in British history. Income tax was raised from 7s to 7s6d in the pound and surtax was levied on those whose incomes exceeded £1,500 a year. Beer went up by 1d a pint, whisky by 1s9d a bottle to 16s; tobacco duty was increased by 3d an ounce and matches by a ½d a box. Postal charges for inland letters went up by 1d to 2½d, and all inland telephone calls by 15 per cent. That same year the 'points' system of rationing was introduced for clothing and tinned meats. Tinned salmon, crab, oranges, pineapples, lemons and so on were not officially rationed because they were almost impossible to get hold of.

In February 1942, Sir Stafford Cripps told the House of Commons that "personal extravagance must be eliminated altogether:" no petrol for pleasure motoring, a cut in the clothing ration and sporting events curtailed. Cigarettes were not officially rationed but tobacconists would often sell only to regular customers (2s4d for twenty). Silk stockings became a thing of the past and women resorted to painting their legs with gravy browning. In 1938 over 33 million pairs of stockings were imported but by 1944 the total had dropped to just 718,000 pairs.

At the beginning of 1945 the weekly basic ration was 4ozs bacon, 2ozs tea, 8ozs sugar, meat to the value of 1s2d, 8ozs of fats, 3ozs of cheese and two pints of milk. In March the milk ration was increased by an extra half pint per person per week, but by May shortages led to reductions in bacon and lard rations. The clothing ration in 1945 was 48 coupons. A man's suit made of utility cloth took 24 coupons, and soldiers being discharged early on medical grounds could make a small fortune by selling their demob outfits. The outfit included a suit that would have cost around £12 in Civvy Street, a shirt worth 25s, two collars, a tie, two pairs of socks, a pair of shoes, a raincoat, and a felt hat. The army valued the whole outfit at £11. On the black market, the price could be upped because the buyer stood to save 56 coupons.

This amusing notice appeared on a shop in south London in September 1939. Had the milkman come for his money?

A one horsepower Pontiac driven by Chelsea sportsman Jack Walsh on 23 September 1939. The photograph was taken to publicise what might be the shape of things to come should petrol rationing be introduced.

The introduction of petrol rationing and a horsepower tax saw many motorists either put their vehicles into store or sell them for scrap. Among what are now collector's items are a Vauxhall 14-Six, an Austin Light 12, a Morris Eight and two Morris Tens.

Petrol Up To 1s. 9½d. Today

By the City Editor

THE price of pool motor spirit is raised today by 1½d. a gallon to 1s. 9½d.—the highest price for 15 years—with the usual surcharges for North and West Scotland, etc. The Government has agreed to the increase, which follows an earlier rise of 2d. a gallon made on October 17.

In a statement issued last night the Petroleum Board, the voluntary organisation of petrol and benzol distributors established at the outset of the war, says that the increase is necessary to offset the increased costs of importing and distributing petrol to which the war has given rise.

The last advance in the retail price of petrol only partly compensated for this rise in costs.

Wet fish was not rationed as such but tinned crab, salmon and the like were almost unobtainable and from November 1941 were included in the points system for tinned foods.

Ration books at the ready. The rationing of basic foodstuffs was introduced in January 1940.

A ration book.

"How does your garden grow?" People were encouraged to rent
allotments and grow their own vegetables.

1 EGG FOR YOU EACH WEEK

AN egg a week may be the "ration" when control comes into force next month. And there is no guarantee of that.

The Ministry of Food stated yesterday that until they have obtained experience of the number of home-produced eggs secured under the new control scheme, and have observed the distributive machinery in operation, it is not possible to state the number of eggs that will be available for each consumer.

They hope that everyone will be able to obtain during July at least four eggs, but no guarantee can be given.

The first allocation of eggs is being made at the beginning of the first week in July, and should be available in the shops

Dig for Victory. LMS employees convert an embankment into allotments. March 1940.

Was this London's highest Dig for Victory? At 110ft above the pavement beans, tomatoes and marrows flourish in a rooftop garden created by LPTB engineer-in-chief, Mr V A M Robertson. August 1943.

"For what we are about to receive." Children of war workers at the Mary Ward Settlement, St Pancras, say Grace before having their morning meal. January 1944.

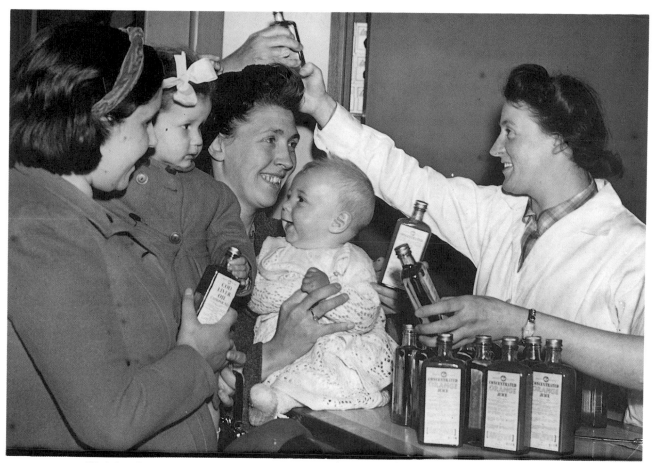

"Drinks all round." Concentrated orange juice arrives from the United States. The photograph was taken at a welfare centre in Tottenham in 1942. *Crown Copyright*

On the whole, the welfare centre at Tottenham (*top pic*) seems to be a far livelier place than the Pheasantry Club.

Mr Duff-Cooper's call for a silent column catches on in this bar. The idea was that anyone caught spreading rumour or dangerous gossip would be fined one penny on the spot which they had to put in the *chatterbox*. All proceeds to the Red Cross.

Be careful
what you say
+ where you
say it!

CARELESS TALK
COSTS LIVES

".... strictly between
these four walls!"

CARELESS TALK
COSTS LIVES

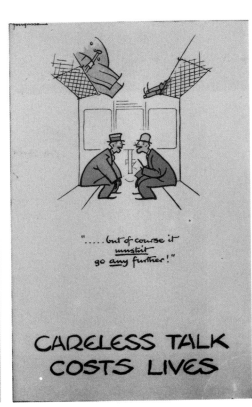

".....but of course it
mustn't
go *any* further!"

CARELESS TALK
COSTS LIVES

Is *Bugs* having his fur stroked or is he being measured for a pastry overcoat? The Duke of Norfolk opened an *Off The Ration Exhibition* at London Zoo in August 1942. The rabbit was one of the stars of the show.

April 1944. Where the holes come from in the seats of small boys' trousers has long been a mystery and non more so than during the war. Here, Miss K Fullylove demonstrates the best way to repair the offending part at a *Domestic Front Exhibition* held at Camden Town.

The *Rinso* mobile emergency unit equipped with its own power and water supply, goes into action in the blitzed areas of east and south London. The WVS collected the clothes and saw to it that they got back to their owners washed and dried.

Clothes rationing followed on from food and fuel. In 1942 the allowance was forty-eight coupons a year; it took fifteen coupons to buy a pair of socks.

Ladies must have thought that Christmas had come early in this Croydon store in September 1941 when sub-standard stockings went on sale — coupon free! In 1938 over 33 million pairs of stockings were imported but by 1944 the total had dropped to 718,000 pairs, forcing many a fashion conscious girl to resort to gravy browning. When the Government reduced imports, they unleashed a new crime wave on the community — silk stocking snatching.

Signs of the times. In the weeks immediately following the Dunkirk evacuation, many expected the Germans to launch an all-out invasion. Two of the steps taken were to remove all signposts from British roads and reduce the size of those at railway stations to ensure that little help was given to an invader.

Sunlight and shadow at St Pancras.

A day at the races? Possibly not, as many racegoers found that the special train to Newmarket was already filled to overflowing. Liverpool Street, April 1942.

Crowds of people wait for trains — often for hours.

Over 1,200 passengers could not get on to the 1.35am train to the south west at Waterloo. Many were still at the station at 11.00am the following day when this photograph was taken. 24 July 1943.

Topical Press photograph from October 1944 showing the first trials of neon lighting on London's Underground in a car running on the District Line.

Children from an East End nursery school take to the road to spend a holiday in the country. August 1943.

Left: Mr Geoffrey Lloyd, Minister of Mines, inspecting a gasbag trailer attached to a London bus. The buses ran on coal gas instead of petrol, and one of the most successful operators was Barton Buses of Chilwell, Nottinghamshire, whose vehicles had, by June 1941, used up 25 million cubic feet of gas and covered 500,000 route miles, saving 75,000 gallons of petrol.

A veteran of earlier conflicts makes his donation to Lord Beaverbrook's appeal for people to give up their aluminium pots and pans for use in the aircraft industry. This photograph was taken at Chelsea where the WVS collected a record amount. However, the whole exercise yielded very little high-grade aluminium.

Stanley Hurn enjoys a pinta. Workers in jobs where the atmosphere was contaminated with a high percentage of lead were allowed two pints of milk a day. Expectant mothers, children and invalids were each allowed a pint a day; the remainder of the population got about two pints a week each.

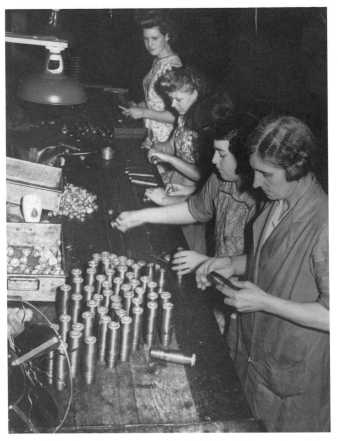

Mrs W Davies (nearest camera) of Charlton helps make anti-aircraft shells in a converted garage. The machinery used in this factory was salvaged from a scrapyard. Mrs Davies is plugging and packing shells.

Hands that do dishes now help with the war effort.

Former London shop assistant Miss R Knight pushes a trolley laden with small calibre anti-aircraft shells.

CANTEEN SERVICE

The new CANTEEN will be OPEN MONDAY NEXT, SEPT. 29th.

Those wishing to have Dinners on that day should purchase their tickets from the Canteen on Saturday Sept. 27th

The following prices will be Charged in the Canteen

Meat 2 Vegetables, Bread	10d & 11d
Fish „ „	10d
Boiled Pudding & Cutard	3d
Milk „ „	3d
Stewed Fruit „	3d
Cakes	1½d & 2d
Tea	per ½ pint 1d
Coffee or Cocoa	„ 1½d

Employees should note that they are expected to provide their own Knife, Fork & Spoon

Making munitions in a private house in Surbiton, April 1943.

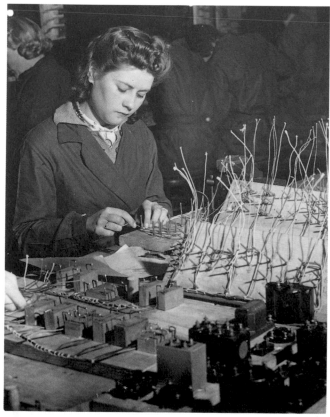

East Ham Technical College, March 1941, was one of a large number of institutions where women trained for munitions work. Here a girl works on cable forms.

Women are at work at the LPTB Workshops, Parson's Green manufacturing concrete bus stops. The photograph is a general view showing the moulds after filling. April 1943.

In order to speed up the output of driver-mechanics for the ATS, a number of women were
sent on training courses to garages and workshops in South London.

In order to speed up the throughput of aerogrammes, the GPO installed date stamping equipment previously used by a
football pools company. The machine could process 13,000 items per hour. November 1942.

August 1941. Men of Austrian, German and Italian origin register for employment at Lion House, Holborn, under the International Labour Force Registration Order for friendly aliens.

Boys chat with an Italian prisoner of war who was one of twenty-five put to work filling in obsolete trench shelters. March 1942.

Mrs Churchill visits a photographic exhibition at Dorland Hall, Regent Street, August 1942. The theme was her husband's visit
to the Middle East.

30 June 1943. Winston Churchill in a jovial mood outside the Mansion House after receiving the Freedom of the City. His daughter, Mary Churchill, seems highly amused at the Premier's attempt to raise his hat whilst simultaneously giving his famous victory sign.

Don't forget that walls have ears!

Bundles for Britain Exhibition at Harrods, January 1942.

Clement Attlee takes tea following the opening of the new Victoria League Hostel in Vauxhall Bridge Road, 14 October 1942.

That's Entertainment

It would be wrong to think that life came to a halt. True, BBC Television had closed down for the duration but there were only a few thousand sets in the country anyway and the vast majority of these were in London. However, nine out of ten homes had a radio set and the re-organized BBC Home Service was to broadcast some classic programmes including *ITMA* (It's That Man Again) staring Tommy Handley; *Band Waggon* staring Arthur Askey and Richard 'Stinker' Murdoch; and *Hi Gang!* with Bebe Daniels and Ben Lyon. Broadcast twice daily was *Worker's Playtime* from factory canteens 'somewhere in England' and for the serious listener there was *The Brains Trust* featuring Professor Cyril Joad, Julian Huxley and A B Campbell.

Dance band music filled much air time, some of the favourites being Billy Cotton, Joe Loss, Jack Hylton and Henry Hall. The popular singers of the day were Vera Lynn, Ann Shelton and Gracie Fields. When the American Forces Network was established, British listeners were treated to the big band sounds of Tommy Dorsey and Glenn Miller; jazz from Benny Carter; the singing talents of Ella Fitzgerald; and a new singing phenomenon named Frank Sinatra. American comedians like Bob Hope, Jack Benny and Red Skelton proved to be popular with Britsh listeners. Of all, it is the music of Glenn Miller that has become synonymous with the war.

Drury Lane, 22 September 1939. Sir Seymour Hicks is in a happy mood as he discusses the itineraries for NAAFI concert parties scheduled to entertain troops stationed with the British Expeditionary Force (BEF).

The first NAAFI concert party to leave for France poses for the press at Victoria Station on 14 November 1939. *Left to right:* Dennis Noble, William Walker (pianist), Claire Luce, Peter Stewart (manager), Sir Seymour Hicks, the *New York Blondes,* Tom Stewart and the *Exquisite Ascots.* Just visible behind Tom Stewart is the conjurer Deveen.

Gracie in London, April 1940, following her return from France where she had been entertaining the troops. Husband Monty Banks is on the right.

30 October 1940. Jean Mackie gives a lunch hour concert at a communal dining centre.

Aldwych Underground Station, October 1940. Members of the public taking shelter from the nightly incursions of the *Luftwaffe* are entertained by an ENSA concert party.

ENSA concert party, Aldwych Underground, October 1940.

"Play it Sam, play it." Sam tickles the ivories above the boarded over swimming pool at the YMCA which was being used as an air raid shelter.

Bud Flanagan and Chesney Allen with bus conductress (and rhyme writer) Joan Chapman. Some of Joan's rhymes were used in Jack Hyltons show Hi-de-hi.

"The big sneeze." Bud Flanagan, Chesney Allen and actor Naunton Wayne attempt to sneeze to order during the BBC Red Cross competition. Despite being plied with snuff, sneezing to order was not that easy. However Bud was first passed the post. April 1941.

Left: Carmen Miranda (alias Tommy Trinder) and the rest of the *Best Bib and Tucker* cast at the London Palladium were regular contributors to the Red Cross Penny-a-Week Fund. Daphne Blake, who collected contributions each week, organised collections among the casts in twenty West End theatres. Tommy Trinder holds the unique record for playing the most West End theatres in one night. During the Blitz, theatre audiences were required to remain in their seats. It was on one such night after the air raid sirens had given out their ominous warning, that Trinder drove from theatre to theatre offering to do a ten minute spot in each. By the time the all clear sounded he had given seventeen separate performances.

"You lucky people!" It's June 1942 and Tommy Trinder begins his tour of Stepney as part of the campaign to establish five hundred war savings street groups. Trinder often described himself as the Mr Woolworth of showbusiness, and, whilst some of his material could on occasions be considered earthy, he never resorted to crudity. From the very start of the war, Trinder went out of his way to entertain service personnel stationed in the United Kingdom. In 1943 he was quite unjustly singled out for criticism in the House of Commons — his 'crime' being not to have worked overseas for ENSA. He did, however, become the first major British star to tour Italy and in 1946 he topped the bill of the last ENSA show to tour bases in the Far East.

Chorus girls at the London Palladium making their weekly contribution to the Red Cross penny-a-week fund. February 1943.

Something For The Boys. Rehearsals for the Cole Porter show in London prior to a Christmas season in Glasgow. December 1943.

Something different for the boys in June 1944. Mrs H Hale not only provided tea and sandwiches for the troops but was not averse to giving inpromptu gigs on her accordian.

A great comedy star caught by the camera in a serious moment. Will Hay was the star of many classic comedy films including *The Goose Steps Out, Oh! Mr Porter* and *Where's That Fire.* He was also a Fellow of the Royal Astronomical Society and, as a sub-lieutenant in the RNVR, taught navigation to hundreds of cadets. December 1942.

The ballet interlude during the Royal Pantomime *Old Mother Red Riding Boots.* The plot so far — The Princess Margaret and the boy have been shrimping whilst the Princess Elizabeth looks on. The sailor (played by Anne Critchen) performs a very ribald hornpipe in which the nurse finally joins but stops when she realises that her behaviour is being observed. Penitent the nurse returns to her stool and asks the Princess Margaret to perform a very ladylike Victorian dance.

Sport

Football was the major spectator sport of the 1930s and the season was only three fixtures old when the League programme was abandoned. In fact the last goal scored in the League before war was declared, was that scored by Ronnie Rooke of Fulham in a match against Luton Town which was not played until the evening of 2 September following a request from the ARP authorities.

On Monday 4 September, daily newspapers carried the news that places of entertainment were closed and all sporting events where crowds were liable to gather, including athletics, greyhound racing, cricket, speedway racing, boxing and football, were cancelled until further notice for fear of heavy casualties in the event of air raids.

The restrictions were soon relaxed and by the third week in October the League began again on a regional basis but with restrictions on ground capacities. London clubs played in the League South 'A' Division and League South 'C' Division for 1939-40, the Southern Regional League in 1940-41, the London League in 1941-42 and the Football League South from 1942-43 onwards.

The war affected the clubs in a number of ways. Highbury was taken over and converted into an ARP centre with a barrage balloon sited on the practice pitch, forcing the *Gunners* to decamp to White Hart Lane to play their home fixtures. A number of grounds also suffered from bomb damage. Highbury took a direct hit from a 1000kg bomb on the training pitch and incendiaries destroyed the North Bank roof. At Upton Park, the home of West Ham United, a VI doodlebug destroyed a large section of the South Bank terracing and the adjoining end of the Main Stand and severely damaged the West Stand, forcing the club to set up offices in Green Street House. Millwall's ground was also damaged, forcing them to play their games at Charlton, whilst Charlton's ground in turn suffered slight damage to the North End.

On 1 June 1940, West Ham and Fulham clashed at Stamford Bridge in one of the semi-finals of the League War Cup, the kick-off being delayed until 6.40pm so that munitions workers could make their way to the game. In front of a crowd of 32,799 fans, West Ham won by 4-3 having allowed Fulham to pull back from 4-0 with two goals from Ronnie Rooke and a single from Viv Woodward. The following week the *Hammers* were in action again, in the final against Blackburn Rovers at Wembley, where the ground capacity for the match was restricted to 43,000

The National Anthems of Britain and France were played by the band of the Irish Guards and the game began.

The first half was dominated by West Ham, Stan Foxall and George Foreman forcing Blackburn's goalkeeper Barron to make a number of Peter Shilton type saves. Barron's luck ran out in the 34th minute, when Foxall and Len Goulden combined to set up George Foreman for a shot at goal. Barron could only parry the shot which rebounded out for Sam Small to run in and score an easy goal.

In 1941-42, Arsenal won the London League championship with 48 points and won their qualifying group in the London War Cup only to be beaten in a semi-final replay at Brentford. The following year, London clubs were playing in the Football League South. Arsenal were on form and took the League Championship and the League South Cup. The Cup Final against Charlton Athletic was played on 1st May in front of 75,000 fans. The *Gunners* were on devastating form and thrashed Charlton 7-1, Reg Lewis scoring four, Ted Drake two and Denis Compton one.

The main problem facing all clubs was that many players had been called up for military service which meant that League games were often played with scratch sides featuring guest players, and on occasions even volunteers from the crowds!

"Knees bend arms stretch!" Charlton Athletic's ground is the scene of activity as youths and men undergo voluntary physical training under a scheme designed to get them fit and keep them fit, until time for them to enter the armed forces. June 1940.

Army supporters, including this lot from the Royal Artillery, were in full force to support their team in a match against England at Selhurst Park. January 1940. *Below:* England goalkeeper Bartram clears from an Army attack.

The Home Guard

On 14th May 1940, Sir Anthony Eden, the Secretary of State for War, broadcast an appeal for men aged between 17 and 65 to form a new force whose prime function would be to guard factories, railways, canals and other vital points, and to oppose enemy paratroops until regular troops could join battle.

Within minutes of Sir Anthony's appeal, the first volunteers were already reporting to police stations to enrol. Initially the new force was to be called the Local Defence Volunteers, though more than one wit re-christened them the "Look, Duck and Vanish".

Among the early instructions issued to the LDV was one concerning the use of shotguns and sporting cartridges. These items were defined as legal weapons for use against enemy paratroops "but only if used by properly enrolled members of the LDV." Therefore one must assume that any ordinary citizen who took a potshot at a passing Nazi was liable to prosecution.

Within two weeks LDV units were mounting armed patrols with a mixture of weapons ranging from sporting guns, clubs, broom-handles, and even Zulu War assegai.

On 23rd July, the LDV was renamed the Home Guard and on the following day the Government announced that the force could now be issued with boots. In August supplies of battle dress uniforms were made available and more importantly rifles and tommy-guns arrived in our ports from America. The Home Guard in every county, every town and village sat up all night waiting to receive their weapons; men and women toiled day and night making them fit for use. Now the Home Guard could transfer 30,000 British type .303 rifles to the rapidly expanding regular army.

Gradually more sophisticated weapons were added to the Home Guard armoury — sten guns, sticky-bombs, Blacker Bombards, Northover Projectors and the superb Browning Automatic Rifle which brought new words like sear, rear-sear, rear-sear retainer and rear-sear retainer-keeper into the Home Guard vocabulary. Churchill urged that the Home Guard be allowed to man light anti-aircraft guns and heavy searchlights. At last the "Look, Duck and Vanish" image of the earlier cynics faded. The Home Guard had come of age.

All training, particularly the handling of weapons, was taken seriously and real danger was never far away. The Molotov Cocktail (a combination of petrol and a wick contained in a glass bottle) was most hazardous to handle during the early days of tuition. The Blacker Bombard was particularly notorious in that its projectiles often failed to explode.

The anti-climax came in August 1944, when the War Office announced that arrangements were being made to stand-down the Home Guard, including anti-aircraft units. In September all manning of rocket projectors and guns became voluntary and on 1st October all operational manning by Home Guard units ceased.

On 3rd December 1944, the Home Guard was officially stood-down and detachments from all over the country took part in a parade through London. As the Home Guard was stood-down, not disbanded, the men and women were not demobilized. Are they therefore, technically, still serving?

A mention ought to be made of the National Defence Company which came into being in 1936 in response to a War Office request for ex-servicemen to enrol for duty in the event of a national emergency. The National Defence Company was mobilized on 24 August 1939 and immediately posted to guard duties at barrage balloon headquarters, petrol and military stores depots, aerodromes, rail and road bridges and so on. This particular force was absorbed into Home Defence battalions of the regular army, though at least one, the 30th Battalion Royal Northumberland Fusiliers, served on garrison duties overseas.

National Defence Corps post by the side of a railway, November 1939. *Collection CJ Hardy.*

Many, unable to join the Home Guard, took up shooting. Here, officers of the Brixton Police practice on the ranges at Bisley. June 1940.

A miniature range on the roof of a London business house where staff practiced their marksmanship. June 1940.

The London Gun Club at Northolt opened its doors to the public on 29 June 1940, offering free instruction to members or prospective members of the LDV. The picture shows Hazel Andrews with her father Mr AJ Andrews.

Two of a series of aircraft silhouettes issued by the War Office to help LDV's and the public identify German troop transports. June 1940. *Left:* Junkers Ju86. *Right:* Junkers Ju52. *Crown Copyright.*

July 1940. A sergeant of the Grenadier Guards puts a squad of the Houses of Parliament LDV through its paces. The unit was formed of peers, MPs and officials. Included in the photograph are *left to right:* Mr Orlando Williams (white jacket) who was an official of the House, the Rt Hon James Stuart MP and Sir James Edmonson.

Stopping enemy tanks. The trailer is playing the part of Hitler's Panzers. Early anti-tank tactics were based on the experiences of those who had served in the International Brigade during the Spanish Civil War.

Left: July 1940. Within the shadow of Big Ben members of the Houses of Parliament LDV drill with P17 Enfeld rifles.

London County Council's LDV drill at County Hall. August 1940.

A detachment of the 1st American Squadron, Home Guard, parade for a photographer from the Keystone Press Agency on 12 November 1940. The unit was about to take part in exercises, along with the Coldstream Guards, and was commanded by General Sir Wade Hayes who had served with General Pershing during the Great War.

Members of a Home Guard unit credited with bringing down an enemy bomber with rifle fire. In reality the bomber had already been mauled by RAF fighters and was flying at very low level. The Home Guardsmen might well have administered the *coup de grâce*.

Bayonet drill for members of the University College Hospital Medical School Home Guard.

The Post Office Home Guard practice rapid rifle fire against an RAF Tiger Moth. July 1941.

"Stand too!" Members of the Port of London Authority unit await the approach of the "enemy" during an exercise somewhere on the waterfront, September 1941.

Was this the chain of command? A guardsman of the Port of London Authority unit takes cover behind a pile of chain. September 1941.

A Northover Projector mounted on a lightweight two-wheel carriage is helped over a style.

Demonstration firing of a Northover Projector, an unattractive looking "but fun to fire" anti-tank weapon.

Saturday afternoon lessons at Victoria House, Leicester Square, where the Women's Home Guard Defence learnt to shoot. Here, a member receives her instructions from Dr Summerskill, who was herself an excellent shot. December 1941.

Mayfair Women's Home Guard Defence throw a Christmas party.

On the right track. Members of the Southern Railway Home Guard in their training school — a converted camping coach.

"Anyone seen the lieutenant's monocle?" The antics of this unit has attracted an audience of small boys and pram-pushing ladies, but it's serious stuff alright. In this exercise the unit has been ambushed and they must take whatever cover they can find.

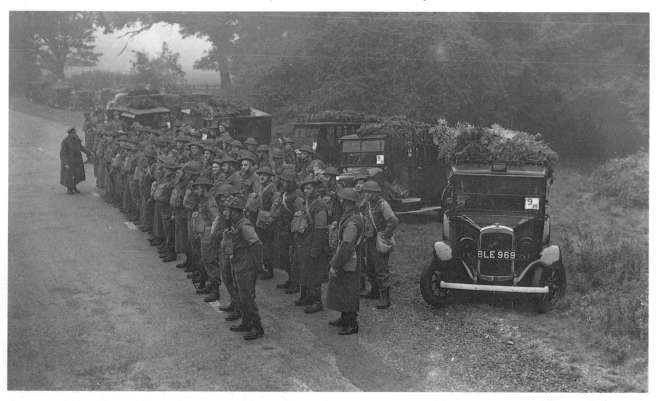

London taxi-cabs figured in the front line of Britain's defences in October 1942 when several hundred drivers, who were all members of the London District Transport Column, Home Guard, took part in a large scale exercise in Greater London. Their job was to resist an invasion force which had established a bridgehead at Southend and were advancing upon London through Epping Forest. Also taking part were hundreds of lorry drivers whose task was to deliver supplies, ammunition and troops to the battle zone.

Home Guardsmen put theory into practice at a street fighting school.

Camouflaged Home Guardsman of the 25th London Battalion.

"Come out with your hands up!" A street fighting exercise in the Wood Street area of the city. Home Guardsmen of the attacking force flush out a defender.

Members of the LMS Home Guard defend a locomotive depot during a local exercise.

Home Guardsmen practice grenade throwing, but only the sergeant has anything worth throwing.

Members of the London Passenger Transport Board Home Guard brush up on their anti-tank skills.

Members of the Home Guard take part in an exercise defending a London station against an attack by 'enemy' paratroops.

The *Tickler Tank* was the brainchild of Colonel Tickler of Maidenhead and constructed out of sheet metal salvaged from scrapyards on a Sunbeam car chassis.

"Come in twenty-three, your time's up!" Rear-admiral Sir Basil Brooke, chief commander of the River Home Guard, with Sir Ralph Glynn MP and Vice-admiral WT James, review patrol craft on the Thames. Members of the unit were given naval ranks and wore a special uniform consisting of a sweater, monkey jacket and yachting cap. There were river patrols operating in other parts of the country including on the Trent in Nottinghamshire but there members wore army uniforms and were given army ranks.

General Sir Frederick Pile, GOC Anti-Aircraft, visits a Home Guard manned light anti-aircraft battery.

A spectacular photograph of a Home Guard ZZ anti-aircraft rocket battery opening fire. Because it was necessary to crew the batteries on a rota system, it was almost impossible for anyone on shift work to take part. Also it was essential that the men who did work on this type of equipment were physically fit and had good eyesight, so as to be able to lift the heavy projectiles for loading and to set the fuses accurately.

Blitz

It was a glorious late summer afternoon on Saturday 7 September 1940, when at 4.56pm London's air raid sirens wailed their ominous warning across the city. As people scurried to the shelters, many would have wondered whether it was a practice alert or the real thing. They did not have long to wait. Within minutes the distinctive drone of unsynchronized aero engines, the crump crump of anti-aircraft gunfire, then the scream and heavy thump of exploding bombs, left no one in any doubt.

Moving up-river from the east came wave after wave of German long-range bombers with a massive fighter escort. Apart from a few fleecy clouds, it was a clear afternoon and the *Luftwaffe* aircrews had no difficulty in locating their targets.

On the ground the bombers left behind a creeping barrage of bombs and incendiaries starting at the Ford Motor Works at Dagenham, then Beckton Gas Works and the Royal Docks. But it was in the East End that all hell broke loose as bombs fell among the densely-populated dockland streets of terraced houses, warehouses and factories.

London's Civil Defence structure was to be tested to the limit. With bombs still falling rescue teams, first aid parties, the police and firefighting services set about their tasks. But for many of them, all their training, no matter how professional it had been, could not have prepared them for the horrors to come. Many of the victims — men, women and children — had been appallingly mutilated, others were literally blown to pieces so that nothing remained; of some there was only a foot, a hand or a piece of raw flesh left. Then there were the victims of bomb blasts. Their bodies often showed no outward signs of injury and they could be mistaken for being asleep, yet quite uncannily their clothes and shoes were sometimes missing having been blown off by the bomb blast leaving the corpses stark naked.

As fires raged in West Ham amid warehouses, oil depots, chemical works and houses, hundreds of firefighting crews were committed to the area. By 6.30pm Lambeth Regional Fire Headquarters had logged nine *conflagrations*, in other words fires needing at least a hundred pumps, but where the situation was such that to all intents and purposes the fires could be classed as out of control. There were nineteen other fires each being attended by thirty pumps, thirty fires each requiring ten pumps and over a thousand fires each requiring one or two pumps.

Few of the regular LFB men would have had experience at fires on this scale — before the war a fire requiring thirty pumps would have made the national newspapers and possibly *Pathe News* at the cinema. Of the AFS crews, eighty per cent had never attended so much as a minor fire let alone a *conflagration*.

The most spectacular of the *conflagrations* was at the Surrey Commercial Docks, where 250 acres of stacked timber was well and truly ablaze. To make matters worse, burning embers were being sucked into the air by the updraught only to fall elsewhere and start new fires.

Problems facing the firecrews were tremendous: roads blocked with debris; water mains destroyed; and communication links with headquarters reduced to relying upon the undoubted bravery of messenger boys and dispatch riders. Firecrews operating close to the docks, though not short of water, had to contend with the hazards created by the burning contents of warehouses. There was at least one pepper fire, as well as paint fires, oil fires, sugar fires, all with their own characteristics and inherent dangers. The crew of the first firefloat to enter the West India Docks had no problem in identifying the characteristics of the fire that they had been deployed to tackle — it was moving towards them. The warehouses on the rum quay were alight from end to end and thousands of gallons of rum had poured into the dock basin creating a sea of liquid fire.

By 6.00pm the bombs and incendiaries had stopped falling and the all-clear sounded. On the ground chaos reigned but the rescue work continued without let up. About two hours later, Lambeth Regional Control were warned that another raid was imminent. A force of about 250 bombers, guided by the fires caused by the first attack, proceeded to drop much of their payload in the same areas.

By now, London's firefighters were totally committed and brigades from as far as Thames Valley and Rugby in the South Midlands were asked to send reinforcements, which when they arrived were committed to helping out in the city of London.

The situation in the East End was now so serious that many of the inhabitants were evacuated. With exit roads blocked by debris and fire, people living in the Silvertown district of West Ham were evacuated by boat. In the Surrey Docks a convoy of vehicles was organised by the WVS to take mothers, children and the elderly to safety before fire cut them off from the rest of London.

On the river, ships were on fire and navigation was hazardous due to a number of 100 tonne dumb barges which were ablaze from end to end and drifting downriver on the ebb tide.

As night descended, the *conflagration* at the Royal Arsenal, Woolwich, was giving cause for concern. The complex had been badly mauled by the first wave of bombers and a number of fires were out of control and threatening to engulf some of the ammunition stores.

Added to this was the fact that many of the water mains within the arsenal had been destroyed and water was having to be relayed from firefloats to the pumps ashore. The fires were eventually contained, water being pumped from the Thames at the rate of 4 tonnes a minute.

The all-clear sounded just before 5.00am on the morning of 8 September. Fire still raged, rescue teams and volunteers searched for survivors and victims, and the bombed-out were led to rest centres where they could collect their thoughts, have a meal and make arrangements for their future.

The official casualty list for the first day and night was 436 men, women and children killed and 1,600 severely injured. It was the first of many casualty lists, for unbeknown to anyone, London was about to endure two months of sustained bombing. The Blitz had begun.

On 15 September the *Luftwaffe* launched two massive daylight assaults on London. The first was challenged by twenty-two RAF fighter squadrons which came as something of a shock to many bomber crews as it was believed that the RAF was running out of aircraft. Harried all the way, the first of the raiders reached the capital around midday, dropped their bombs and turned for home only to be savaged on the way back.

In the early afternoon our radar stations located another massive attack developing. Hurricanes and Spitfires which were vectored to meet the attack tore into the fist two waves scattering the Heinkels and Dorniers. The third wave of bombers reached the target area but high above London they were suddenly pounced upon by 300 fighters. In all 31 RAF fighter squadrons were engaged.

September 15 had been chosen by the *Luftwaffe* High Command as the day upon which the RAF would finally be smashed as an effective fighting force and the British Government brought to the peace table by the devastation of

London. The *Luftwaffe* had seriously underestimated British fighter strength and the resolve of both the British Government and the civilian population. Now celebrated as Battle of Britain Day, the action fought on 15 September broke the back of the *Luftwaffe's* daylight offensive, and was to lead to the postponement of Operation Sea Lion (the invasion of Britain) and result in a change in German strategy.

The *Luftwaffe* now turned to night bombing, a realistic appreciation of the fact that their fighter arm lacked the strength and range to be able to protect the bombers from the RAF.

Mid-November saw the implementation of the *Luftwaffe's* change in tactics by extending the Night Blitz to the provinces. On the night of the 14th Coventry was raided by 552 long-range bombers in an attack lasting ten hours. So devastating was the raid, that the government lifted restrictions on the media in naming a bombed town, and full coverage was allowed. The image of the city, with a third of its centre completely destroyed, including its cathedral, was presented to

the world and aroused strong feelings against Nazi Germany. What was not reported was that the local authorities almost lost control of the situation and troops called in to help clear the rubble were also there to maintain order.

Before the end of November, Liverpool, Southampton and Birmingham had been subjected to heavy raids. In December, weather conditions were such that for fifteen nights the *Luftwaffe* were unable to get into the air. However, there were eleven major raids and five moderately heavy attacks. London suffered three major attacks and twelve light raids. Liverpool, Birmingham, Leicester and Portsmouth also suffered, as did Sheffield.

But things were not going entirely the *Luftwaffe's* way. From October to December 1940, of 384 bombers lost, only 140 were attributed as being destroyed by enemy action. The others were lost through non-combatant causes such as bad landings on inadequately equipped French airfields or training accidents.

To make matters worse in Europe, relations between Germany and Russia were deteriorating and the Balkans was a

By December 1938 one hundred air raid sirens had been installed in the metropolitan area. The photograph shows the siren installed on the roof of Snow Hill Police Station. In the background are St Paul's Cathedral and the Old Bailey.

powder keg of trouble. In December, Hitler issued orders for the invasion of Russia, and the German military planners were asked to prepare a quick campaign that would rapidly destroy the Soviet command structure and capture as much of Russia's economic resources as possible. To achieve this the *Luftwaffe* would have had to take aircraft from operations against Britain.

From the beginning of January to the end of May 1941, the *Luftwaffe* kept up its assault on Britain. On the night of 11-12 January, 137 long-range bombers attacked London dropping 144 tonnes of high explosives and over 21,000 incendiaries. The most serious incidents of the night occurred at Liverpool Street and Bank Stations. At Bank Station a direct hit caused the booking hall and the roof of the central gallery to collapse, creating what became known as the largest crater in London.

The next major attack on London did not occur until the night of 8-9 March, when 125 bombers dropped 130 tonnes of high explosive and over 24,000 incendiaries. The most notable incident of the night was at Buckingham Palace where the

North Lodge took a direct hit. In a second incident two bombs crashed through the roof of the Rialto Cinema in Coventry Street and plummeted into the *Café de Paris* which was located in the basement. One of the bombs exploded killing two members of a jazz band, the head waiter, the manager and thirty diners. The other bomb failed to detonate.

On 21 June 1941, the eve of the German attack on Russia, the combat strength of the *Luftwaffe* was 4,882 aircraft of which 1,511 were bombers — 200 less than in May 1940. More than half the bomber force was committed to the East.

Attacks on Britain continued, but few large-scale raids could be mounted. By January 1942 the *Luftwaffe* front line squadrons were so desperate for crews that their training courses were cut by one month. By February the quartermaster general's office was no longer in a position to forecast the availability of new aircraft or spares.

Rates of production were not keeping pace with losses as most of the aircraft industry was still working a peacetime

In November 1939, the Germans claimed that the Port of London had been brought to a virtual standstill due to the effectiveness of their mine warfare tactics. This photograph was one of a number issued to counteract their claim and shows the neutral Belgian vessel *Prince De Liege* being unloaded. The port remained in operation throughout the war.

shift of eight hours a day instead of round the clock.

During 1942-43, there were less than thirty raids on London, but 1944 opened with a period now known as the Little Blitz. The *Luftwaffe* had managed to collect a hotchpotch of 550 aircraft in northern France but many of the crews were untrained and a pathfinder unit had to be employed. There were light raids mounted on the 3rd and 14th January and on the 21st two waves totalling 447 aircraft were launched. The attack failed mainly due to poor navigation and only 32 tonnes of bombs fell on London, the rest being scattered far and wide across the south east. For several months the attacks continued but the force eventually ceased to be viable having dropped from 695 aircraft in December 1943 to just 144 operational planes by May 1944.

At 3.50am on 13 June 1944, the London area air raid sirens warned of an impending attack and anti-aircraft batteries went into action against a single aircraft which crashed a few minutes later on open land at Barking. About thirty minutes later a second plane crashed but this time it came down in a populated area causing damage and casualties.

It was two or three days before it was fully realized that the *Luftwaffe* was not suffering from a terminal case of bad workmanship but had deployed a new weapon, a pilotless flying bomb, the VI, which carried a 1000kg warhead.

Throughout June the VI offensive averaged about a hundred launchings a day, and though about half were brought down by the combined efforts of RAF fighter planes and anti-aircraft batteries, the remainder got through to crash down somewhere within the Greater London area. On 21 June, the anti-aircraft batteries were moved out of London to the North Downs, directly below the VI's flight paths.

On the 18 June, the most famous, or infamous, VI incident of the war occurred when the Guards Chapel took a direct hit whilst a service was in progress; one hundred and nineteen people were killed, and over a hundred were seriously injured.

In July, the anti-aircraft guns were resited to the coast, where, by sheer weight of firepower, they destroyed well over half of all incoming VIs. By the end of August, the British Second Army had overrun the VI launch sites in the Pas-de-Calais, forcing the Germans to adopt the practice of air-launching the weapons from Heinkel IIIs. Over seven hundred VIs were air-launched, but many exploded upon release, taking their mothership with them. Others reached their targets not only in London but as far north as Manchester and Oldham where twenty-seven people died in one explosion.

On 8 September 1944, a mysterious explosion destroyed a part of Chiswick and Epping. The first V2 had landed. The V2 forty-five foot long ballistic missile, weighing fourteen tonnes, was launched from mobile platforms and it travelled at supersonic speed which meant that it had landed and exploded before anyone heard it arrive! It was too high and fast for any RAF plane to intercept or anti-aircraft battery to engage. In all 518 V2s fell on London, killing 2,724 people and seriously injuring 6,000 others. On 25 March 1945, the last V2 fell, landing near Orpington. A few hours later the last VI came down, falling on Chislehurst.

Admiral Evans, ARP Commissioner for Greater London, watches a firefighting demonstration at the Surrey Commercial Docks.

With the fall of France came fears of imminent invasion and air attacks — the 'Phoney War' was over. *Left:* Children chat with the driver of their evacuation train. *Right:* Evacuees leave Islington, July 1940.

Pupils of Burlington School, Wood Lane, Shepherds Bush clean shoes to raise money to buy comforts for troops. Oxford, June 1940.

Bombs fall in the London area: damage to shops in East Ham, August 1940. This photograph
was originally banned from publication by the censor.

"Danger UXB!" City workers are allowed through, the merely curious are turned away. Unexploded bombs were still
something of a novelty in August 1940 — it would soon wear off!

London is now well and truly in the front line.

Black Saturday, 7 September 1940.

Daylight brought little respite for the fire and rescue services.

The fire is out but the task of salvaging everything usable is only just beginning.

Home Guardsmen lend a hand, helping people salvage their belongings. 8 September 1940.

The queue for water. It was not uncommon for water-mains to be destroyed during a raid and one alternative source of supply was the AFS static tanks.

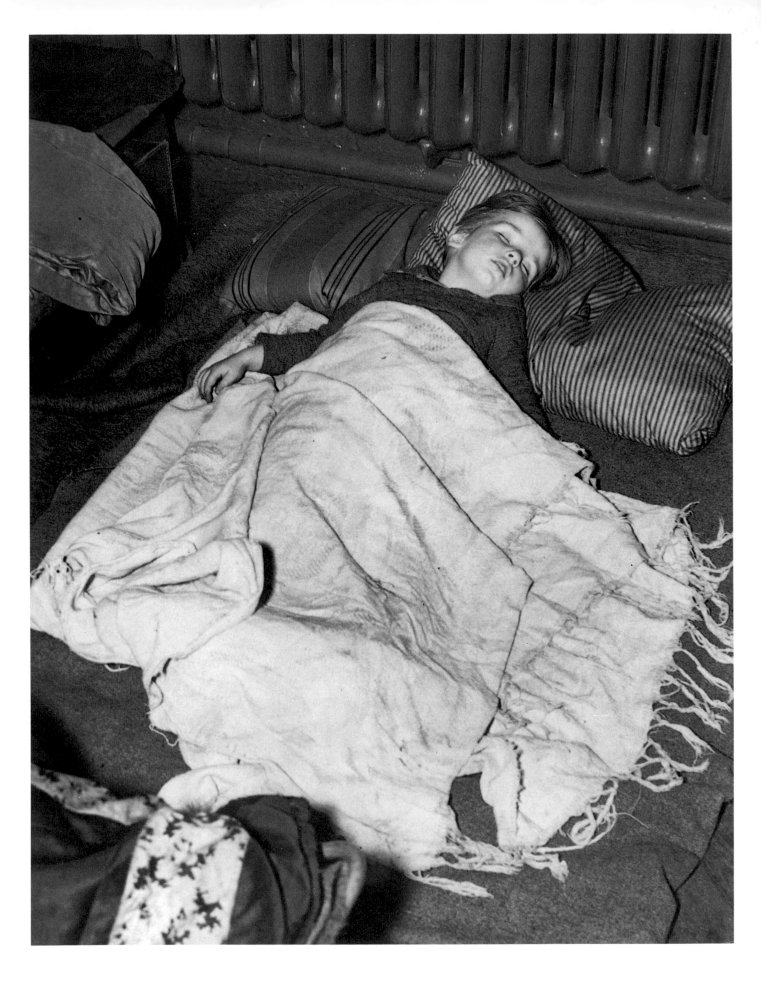

After their house had been destroyed by a bomb, home for this little boy and his family was a school hall. September 1940.

Homeless people from the East End move into a block of luxury flats in the West End. On the whole it was not a successful experiment. September 1940.

Children of one of the eight families using a shelter built beneath a mansion in South East London get ready for school.

Tram wrecked by bomb blast, South London, 9 September 1940.

Wrecked trams at Blackfriars. The censor has erased the shop signs from the buildings behind the leading tram.

Damage in the Portman Street area. The edge of a bomb crater can be seen in the right hand foreground of the picture, in front of the bus.

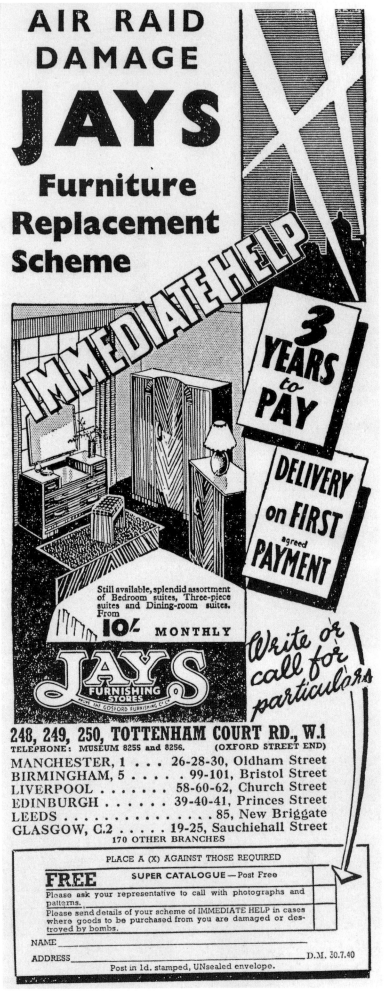

Pioneer Corps and Royal Engineer troops demolish damaged buildings.

Damage in Saville Row. This photograph was banned from publication.

Unsafe buildings in Cannon Street are demolished. St Paul's Cathedral is in the background.

Lieutenant Robert Davies tackles an unexploded bomb in the grounds of the German Hospital in London. It was not until May 1940 that Bomb Disposal Sections were officially sanctioned, each consisting of one officer, a sergeant and fourteen other ranks. Davies found fame in dealing with a Type 17SC1000 unexploded bomb that had come to rest near the clock tower of St Paul's. The bomb was fitted with a booby-trapped fuse, and because considerable damage would be done to the cathedral should it explode, it was decided to physically remove it and deal with it elsewhere. The bomb was dragged from its hole by two lorries, loaded on to one of them, then driven by Davies out of the City. Davies was the first serviceman to be awarded the George Cross.

An incendiary bomb from an odd angle. This particular device is a 1kg incendiary, approximately 2 inches in diameter and 13½ inches in length. The incendiary portion consisted of a cylinder of magnesium alloy with an incendiary filling. To this was rivetted a conical steadying vane with three fins, usually painted green. They were packed in cannisters, each containing thirty-six bombs, which opened after leaving the aircraft so as to scatter them over a wide area — the results could be quite devastating. On average several tens of thousands of incendiaries would be dropped during a heavy raid, but on the night of 10-11 May 1941 a grand total of 86,173 fell on London. In a raid lasting just over six hours, 507 aircraft delivered their payloads, which also included 711 tonnes of HE bombs, on a concentration point to the north of the Thames from Tower Bridge to Stepney, West Ham, Bethnal Green and Leyton, causing many large fires and palls of smoke rising over 10,000 feet into the air. *Crown Copyright.*

Left: A battered but still recognisable Union Jack flies over bomb-scarred ruins. September 1940.

It could be described as one of our secret weapons. The mobile canteen brought tea and hot food when it was most needed — and often whilst the bombs were still falling.

The Blitz brought with it another series of evacuations.

"Hello mummy." Children evacuated to the United States take part in a 3,000 mile two-way Trans Atlantic broadcast. The three were Neville Whittaker, aged 7, who, grinning broadly, obliged his father back in London by snorting like a pig: listening in are his sister Rona, aged 9, and his younger brother Allan, aged 5.

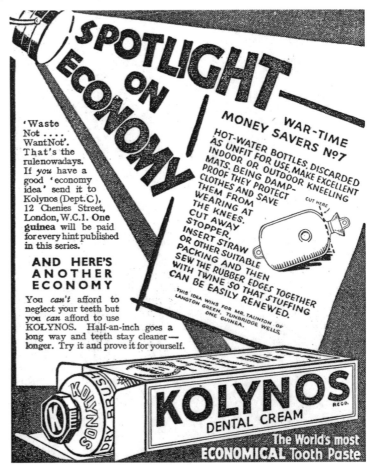
113

"Up down, up down." Daily toothbrush parade for London evacuees at Aldingbourne, Essex.

London schoolchildren at Styal, Cheshire, where they attended the village school.

The evacuation procedures of late 1940 were often chaotic. There was no element of compulsion but help was given in the form of travel vouchers and billeting certificates to those who made their own arrangements. The under-fives were being evacuated by the WVS, schoolchildren by the LCC, and there were different offices depending on whether or not children were to be accompanied, whether billets had already been arranged or not, and so on. It could be a frustating experience for a family attempting to evacuate several children.

Two young evacuees are reassured by a friendly bus conductress at the start of their journey out of the capital. At the start of the Blitz in September 1940 there had been over 500,000 children of school age in the London area.

Comfort comes in the shape of dolls and cuddly toys for these young girls awaiting evacuation by train. Throughout the war the railways as a whole moved three-quarters of a million evacuees out of London on 481 special trains, and a further 1,864 additional trains carried those who had made their own arrangements.

Back to the Blitz! Help is soon at hand for a civilian injured during a daylight attack in October 1940. Note the damaged bus in the background.

Another badly damaged bus. By October LPTB had so many buses, trolleybuses and trams out of action that vehicles were brought in from towns and cities all over the country. Even scrapyards were ransacked for anything that could be made serviceable or used for spares. The censor has obliterated shop signs.

A sad end to a Humber Snipe. The photograph was refused publication on three occasions and did not pass censorship until 11 November 1940.

Police seal off the area after a bomb fractured a gas main during a daylight attack. The photograph was banned from publication by the Press & Censorship Bureau.

The troglodyte world of the Tube shelters.

Bedtime in an underground shelter.

AIR RAIDS

SANIZAL DISINFECTANT

FOR

EMERGENCY

SANITATION

St Mathew's Hospital hit during a raid on the night of 8 October 1940. There were two main attacks on London in the morning and another commencing at around 11.00pm. The daylight raids resulted in 63 people killed and 197 injured, the casualties for the night raid were 138 deaths and 178 injured. There was a major fire at Hays Wharf, Tooley Street, but it was eventually contained and extinguished.

Damage at a London orphanage. October 1940.

Quick check-up at a Red Cross First Aid Post in a Tube shelter. November 1940.

A reception in a bombed house for Flying Officer JC Martin RAF and Miss Ena Squire-Brown following their wedding at St George's Church, Forest Hill. Here the bride leaves for the church.

Their Majesties pay a visit to one of the Tube shelters. November 1940.

Another visitor to the Underground was the Lord Mayor of London, Sir George Wilkinson, where he presented a cheque for £20,000 from his Air Raid Distress Fund to the Minister of Food, Lord Woolton. November 1940.

A Bedford articulated furniture lorry lifted by the blast wave of a bomb. The censors had originally painted out all background detail. November 1940.

Signs of a misspent youth? Thurston's of Leicester Square was the famous home of billiards and snooker. November 1940. Note the names on the boards.

Metal salvaged from blitzed buildings is collected in a London park for sorting and recycling.

St Paul's rises majestically above the scenes of destruction.

The damage around St Paul's. 1941.

The view from St Paul's in 1941, looking east-south-east up Cannon Street.

St Pancras station suffered on several occasions. On 7 November 1940 a platform and the booking hall were badly damaged and in May 1941 a direct hit blew out most of the glass in the arched roof and opened up a gaping hole in the ground that exposed the track of the Metropolitan line running below. The photograph shows repairs well under way.

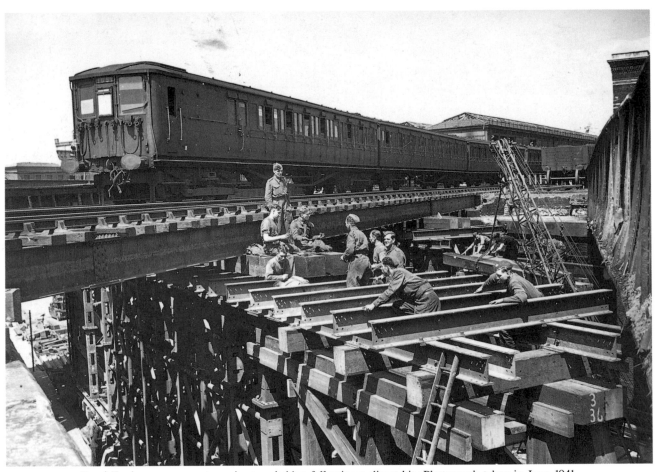

Royal Engineers carry out repairs to a bridge following a direct hit. Photograph taken in June 1941.

Business as usual. A liveried porter stands outside the Dorchester Hotel.

Not released until some months after the event was this photograph of the damage at Bank Station which suffered a direct hit during the raid of the night of 11-12 January 1941. The station took a direct hit in the booking hall which caused the roof to collapse resulting in 35 deaths. Liverpool Street Station was also hit resulting in 43 killed and eighteen others died when a bus took a direct hit. In the photograph troops from the Pioneer Corps and the Royal Engineers have the grim task of clearing debris.

Another view of the destruction at Bank Station which was also witheld from publication. When the bomb exploded in the booking hall, the blast was funnelled down the escalator shaft causing it to collapse, and blowing a number of passengers off the platform into the path of an oncoming train. Although the train's automatic brakes were engaged it was too late for some of those blown into its path. A rescue party arrived from Liverpool Street and within three hours most of the dead and injured had been taken away. In order to get road traffic flowing again a bridge was thrown across what was known as 'the largest crater in London' and it was officially opened by the Lord Mayor on 3 February. By May the roadway had been repaired and the bridge removed.

Another witheld photograph this time showing damage sustained at King's Cross main line station. In November 1940 King's Cross Low Level was hit and damage was inflicted upon offices and a repair shop resulting in fourteen killed and twenty-eight injured.

Members of a rescue party don masks prior to beginning the grim task of searching debris for casualties.
The men would often still be at work when the next raid started, though most of the living were usually freed within a
matter of hours. One girl on Merseyside remained buried for over four days before being released.

Police, Civil Defence workers, and members of the Home Guard assist in Gurney Street
off the New Kent Road.

Bomb damage in the suburbs, August 1942. Note the brick surface shelters in the roadway.

"........but for Heaven's sake don't say I told you!"

CARELESS TALK COSTS LIVES

Aid for animals. The PDSA care for pets from the blitzed areas.

Safe from the blitz. London evacuees at Swindon Road School, Cheltenham, tackle the mysteries of domestic science, 1944.

On the night of 12/13 June 1944, the first V1 flying bombs landed in parts of London and the home counties. For about two weeks, V1s were launched at the rate of a hundred a day, of which about half reached the intended target area whilst others succumbed to our fighters and anti-aircraft guns. The photograph dates from June 1944 and shows little Barbara James being brought out of her house which had been damaged by a flying bomb.

Flying bomb damage in Islington. Though the houses have suffered, the surface shelters have survived.

The V1 threat was reduced when the Allied ground forces overran the launch sites. This example was put on display at Rootes, Piccadilly. In the foreground are two wire bound tanks, part of the pressurised fuel system for the Argus As 014 pulse jet.

Even more deadlier than the V1, and against which little could be done once the weapons were launched, was the V2 ballistic missile. Attaining supersonic speeds in flight to the target, there was no warning, just a single large explosion which levelled whole city blocks, followed by the screeching sound of the rocket's arrival. On one rare occasion a British fighter squadron happened by chance on a V2 rocket just seconds after launch and blasted it out of the sky. This photograph illustrates a V2 rocket being prepared for launching from its mobile carrier vehicle.

The scene of the explosion after London's first V2 had landed in London at Chiswick.

Rescue workers at Farringdon Street, London, after a V2 rocket had fallen.

A general view of Farringdon Street following a V2 attack.

Hitting Back

It would be impossible to include all regular, territorial and auxiliary military units with a London connection as there are scores of them, including The Honourable Artillery Company, The Inns of Court Regiment, London Scottish, The Household Cavalry Regiment, and so on. This section pays tribute to the men and women of the armed forces and Merchant Navy, and with only one or two exceptions the photographs have some direct relevance to London.

Also included are photographs of our Allies, the Americans, Free French, Czechs and Poles as well as several pictures devoted to Dominion and Colonial forces.

The night photographs of anti-aircraft batteries and searchlight units in action are particularly evocative of the period. As Winston Churchill once told Sir Frederick Pile, GOC Anti-Aircraft, "Keep on shooting away regardless." It reassured the civilian population. But what goes up, must often come down. An example of which occurred to an aquaintance of mine who was leading a squad of troops through a wood, miles from anywhere, when they were suddenly 'strafed' with 50-calibre bullets. They had been fired by an aircraft several miles away and, having been 'spent', fell back to earth. Fortunately there was only one casualty.

Heinkel He111P bombers on a training flight before the outbreak of war in 1939. The He111 was the mainstay of the *Luftwaffe* bomber arm for most of the war, being heavily employed in the Blitz in 1940 and 1941. *Courtesy Imperial War Museum.*

Anti-aircraft battery "somewhere in London" August 1939. The guns were accompanied by other equipment including height and range finders and attracted large crowds of sightseers. Drills were often carried out with the crews wearing their gas masks.

A mobile 3·7 inch quick firing anti-aircraft gun of the 1st Anti-Aircraft Division about to commence firing.
The 3·7 inch could lob a 28½lb shell up to a height of 32,000 feet and by 1940-41 was the mainstay of
Anti-Aircraft Command under Lieutenant-General Sir Frederick Pile. At the climax of the Battle of Britain
in September 1940, the 1st AA Division had 199 heavy guns with which to defend the capital.

Gunners set up sandbagged emplacements in a London park.

Right: A mobile 3·7 inch AA gun in position on a bomb site near St Paul's Cathedral.

Below: 'Keep shooting away regardless' was Winston Churchill's order to Sir Frederick Pile. The battery in Hyde Park in action.

Winston Churchill visits a mixed battery in the London area in October 1941.

The Prime Minister and Mrs Churchill watching ATS girls work the predictor at a mixed AA battery.

Vergeltungswaffe Eins or Reprisal Weapon 1, The Fieseler Fi 103 cruise missile. Over 30,000 were built, mainly by Volkswagen and Mittelwerke. It was ramp-launched from sights on the continent. The attacks commenced shortly after D-Day. In July 1944 III Gruppe des Kampfgeschwaders 3 commenced air launching these missiles from bases in Holland, Heinkel He IIIH's launching over 1,200 at targets in Britain. From the aircrew's point of view it was a dangerous operation, KG 53 losing twelve aircraft in two missions from Fi 103's detonating shortly after take off. The Vl cruised at 400mph at 2,500 feet, and many were accounted for by the combined defences of Anti-Aircraft guns, the balloon barrage and fast low level fighters. Here we see a portion of the inner defence ring around the capital in action on the night of 19 June 1944.

In the middle of January 1941, the Air Officer Commanding, Balloon Command, was asked to consider a suggestion that the flying of balloons could be completely carried out by members of the Women's Auxiliary Air Force (WAAFs), despite the fact that the manning of balloons for 24 hours a day, frequently in the most appalling weather conditions, required physical strength not generally possessed by women. However, there had been a number of technical improvements to equipment, including the mechanization of some aspects of handling balloons. Thus, one wet, cold morning in April 1941, twenty WAAF volunteers attended their first course at Cardington. By the end of June, the women had proved their worth and Sheffield was chosen as the site for the first full-scale experiment. On the success of the experiment the whole manning of Balloon Command now rested.

In July, eight women crews took over D Flight of 939 Squadron, and by the end of the year all balloons except those on isolated sites had been taken over by the WAAF.

Searchlights probe the night sky for the enemy. A barrage balloon is caught in the spill of one of the lights.

Searchlights in a park, scanning the sky as another incoming bombing raid threatens the city.

The four-gun turret armed Boulton Paul Defiant enjoyed considerable success against the enemy when it first entered combat over Dunkirk. However, the German pilots soon gained the measure of the Defiant; it lacked a forward firing armament and its manoeuvrability left much to be desired. Losses mounted in August 1940 and the 264 "Madras Presidency" Squadron was badly mauled. The Defiant was withdrawn and converted to the nightfighter role in which it once again enjoyed a measure of success.

Clipped, cropped and clapped. To enable the Spitfire Mk V to compete with the FW 190 at low altitude, the wing tips were clipped to provide a higher rate of roll, the Merlin engine's supercharger rotor was cropped to provide better acceleration, and they were clapped because they were converted from aircraft that had already seen service. This Mk VB was equipped with two 20mm cannon and four .303 machine guns.

"Squadron scramble!" Pilots of 312 Czech Squadron run to their Hurricanes. Formed at Duxford in August 1940 they took part in the defence of London during the latter stages of the Battle of Britain. The top scoring pilot of the Battle was a Czech, Sergeant Joseph Frantisek, who flew with 303 Polish Squadron.

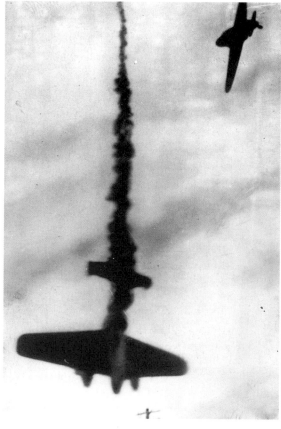

The end of a German bomber.

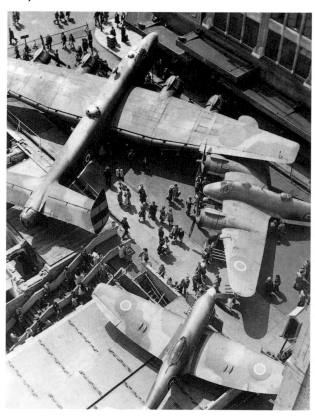

Exhibition of British aircraft in Oxford Street during August and September 1945.

17 Bf 110 Zestorer, as intended to deal with RAF fighters and protect the bombers, having greater endurance than the German single engine fighters, but despite having an undeniably lethal forward armament of four 7.9mm MG17 machine guns and twin 20mm FFs it was no match for the more nimble RAF fighters: during August, 120 were lost, with a further 83 by the end of September and they were withdrawn to reconnaissance and fighter bomber roles. These losses proved particularly embarrassing to Reichsmarshall Goering who had claimed invincibility for his Zestorergruppen in the skies of Britain. This plane crashed within the Borough of Edmonton.

The Anderson shelter had a reputation for being able to survive almost anything apart from a direct hit. This Anderson took a direct hit in the shape of a crashing Messerschmitt Bf109 fighter. Miraculously the shelter's three occupants survived the impact. The railways as a whole transported 66,000 Anderson and Morrison shelters into London for use by those unable or unwilling to be evacuated away from the bombing.

Wrecks of shot down German aircraft were salvaged for valuable scrap during the Battle of Britain and the metal was utilized by the British aircraft industry.

This Messerschmitt Bf109 fighter, disabled in a dog fight, has made a wheels-up landing in a ploughed field in Kent. Note the numerous bullet holes in the fuselage. This type of fighter proved to be a formidable adversary for the RAF's Spitfires and Hurricanes during the Battle of Britain and has entered the annals of aerial warfare as one of the greatest combat aircraft of all time.

On 11 September 1940, Heinkel HeIIIH-3 No 5680, during a sortie to bomb London Docks, was damaged by AA fire and then set upon by Spitfires of 92 Squadron. The Heinkel jettisoned its bombs and crash-landed at Burmarsh. The crew set fire to the plane before they were captured.

The Regia Aeronautica arrived in Belgium in mid-September 1940 to avenge the increasing RAF bomber raids on Italy, and to participate in what had a short time before seemed an inevitable German victory. On 1 November, the Corps Aereo Italiano made a major attack on convoys off Lowestoft and Harwich but received a drubbing at the hands of the RAF. This Fiat BR20M was set upon by Hurricanes of 46 and 257 Squadrons and, badly shot up, crashed at Tangham Forest, Bromeswell, Suffolk.

In November 1940, this Heinkel III of KG55 participating in a raid on London crashed at Matlock Gardens, Hornchurch. After failing to locate its assigned targets in the capital it had released its bombs blind and turned for home, when it received a direct hit on the tail from AA fire and was brought down.

As more and more German aircraft were shot down during the Battle of Britain and large numbers of airmen captured, scenes such as this one at a London railway station became a familiar sight.

This is all that remains of a Junkers Ju88A-5 which crashed in
a garden in Denmark Hill, Wimbledon.

This Junkers Ju88A-5 of 8/KG77 was hit by AA fire during the big raid on London of 16-17 April
1941 and, plunging to earth in a shallow dive it struck the roof of a house in Campden Hill Road,
Kensington, and disintegrated.

Soldiers guard the wreckage of the Junkers Ju88A-5 in Campden Hill Road, Kensington. The crew, Leutnant G Sissimato, Unteroffizers W Meissler and G Abell and Gehrfreiter P Schumann all baled out and were taken prisoner.

The Battle of Britain is and has been won but the war goes on and the night blitz is yet to end. A shot-down Messerschmitt Bfl09E fighter is exhibited outside the Guildhall to aid London's War Weapons Week, May 1941. The Messerschmitt Bfl09E was capable of 348 mph and armed with two 7.9mm machine guns above the engine, two 20mm cannons in the wings and one 20mm cannon fired through the propellor.

The remains of the Messerschmitt Me110, flown to Britain by Rudolf Hess, were exhibited in towns and cities throughout the country.

Did you **MACLEAN** your teeth to-day?

It's the best girls!

Obtainable
everywhere
6ᴰ, 10½ᴰ & 1/6

MACLEANS
PEROXIDE
TOOTH PASTE

Remember
to include a
tube in
his parcel
this week

Disused RAF aero-engines for sale at an East Ham scrapyard, 1943.

Territorials of the London Scottish undergo rifle inspection.

Territorials of the Queen's Westminsters include actors Frank Lawton (end of line) and next to him Guy Middleton.

157

Home for Christmas 1939. A soldier and a sailor head north from Euston.

Home from the BEF, February 1940.

Left: Back to the unit. An artilleryman says farewell.

The last days of the siege of Dunkirk. Soldiers of the BEF take on the dive-bombers.

Above: Polish sailors take part in the Lord Mayor's Show in November 1941, when Allied contingents marched through the city.

Top right: Her Majesty Queen Elizabeth presents new Colours to the Saskatoon Light Infantry, a Canadian regiment. *Crown Copyright.*

Right: Sergeant Neil W Butler of Wisconsin and Sergeant Woodrow W Jorgensen of Chicago, join in the paper salvage campaign, May 1942.

Bastille Day, July 1942. Free French commandos parade through London and were inspected by General de Gaulle at Wellington Barracks.

London burns. Taken during the Blitz.

Bomb damage around the Temple area.

Damage around St Paul's.

Hitting back. Anti-aircraft rocket launcher.

Hitting back. A Spitfire VB of 303 Polish Squadron flown by Squadron Leader Jan Zumbach who led the squadron from May — December 1942. The aircraft carries Zumbach's distinctive Donald Duck insignia and also sports the crestof the Kosciuszko Squadron of the Polish Air Force.

Barrage balloon crewed by WAAFs.

Pay day for WAAFs at a balloon site.

As part of the defence of the Thames Estuary and Port of London areas, balloons were
flown from converted fishing vessels and barges.

Women munitions workers.

A nice uniform but hardly official.

Summer in the city 1941.

Against a background of bomb damaged buildings a London Fire Brigade appliance
is prepared for duty.

The Milestones Club, Kensington, was opened by the American Red Cross to look after members of the US forces in this country. The photograph shows the information bureau at the club. The soldiers are Private First Class L Mouk from Oneida, New York, Private First Class H Bradt of Schenectady, New York, Sergeant JA Kissell of Oceanside, New York, Corporal EJ Marone of Philadelphia and Private Richard Law of Brooklyn.

A reception for a contingent of Indian troops at India House. On the right, Major Mahoumed Akbar Khan Jez Nirzaudin explains to Lady Chelmsford the various decorations of Risaldar Major Mahoumed Ashraf Khan.

"G'day sport." Mr SM Bruce, High Commissioner for Australia, opens a club for men of the Australian Imperial Force, at Australia House in the Strand. At the club the men could get free paper to write home on and catch up with news from back home through copies of Australian newspapers. Everything was done to make the men feel at home. Mrs Bruce serves the tea but one can't help thinking that the boys could do with a beer!

A 9.2 Howitzer in action. Every member of the gun's crew has a specialised job to do — and does it fast!

Men and Women with
WILLS TO WIN
are smoking
GOLD FLAKE
MADE OF PURE VIRGINIA TOBACCO
BY W. D. & H. O. WILLS

The Princess Elizabeth changes a wheel during training at an ATS Training Centre, 1945.

With the ATS in the Southern Command. The gardening squad goes on duty during a break from their normal duties.

Training for duties in the NAAFI, May 1941.

Squad drill at a London depot for NAAFI girls, March 1942.

Sir Bede Clifford *(left),* Governor of Mauritius, hands a cigarette box and cheques totalling £161,000 to the First Lord of the Admiralty Mr AV Alexander. The cigarette box was for the wardroom of HMS *Mauritius,* the cheques went towards helping to pay for her construction. *Crown Copyright.*

Left: Captain TM Jarvis visits Compton Street School, Goswell Road, which had 'adopted' his coaster. 1943.

The Canadian-built merchantman *Fort Dease Lake* photographed in August 1943. Of the forty officers and men of the Merchant Navy serving aboard, twenty were from the London area including, Charlton, Woolwich, Catford, Hammersmith, Deptford, Balham, Acton, Bethnal Green, Euston and Barnes. Other members of the crew were drawn from as far afield as Ayrshire (second mate), Beverley (master), Tippereray (second radio officer), Brighton (chief steward) and Preston (chief cook).

Signalman Alf Fitzgerald of Summer House, Devons Road, Bow, arrives home after five years in German captivity. His mother is cutting his birthday cake, made five years previously. Apparently it was still in good condition. May 1945.

Victory

At Remagen on 7th March 1945 the US 9th Armoured Division seized the only bridge still standing over the Rhine and within hours had pushed three corps of the Twelfth Army Group into a bridgehead nearly ten miles deep on the opposite bank. To the south the Third and Seventh Armies breached the Siegfried Line and on the 23 March crossed the Rhine at Oppenheim. That same day under Montgomery's overall command the Second British Army, the First Canadian Army, the First Allied Airborne Army and the Ninth US Army crossed the Rhine near Wesel.

In the east the Red Army was only 35 miles from Berlin and advancing into Hungary and Austria. On 21 April, Hitler's birthday, Berlin came under direct Russian artillery fire for the first time and their advance forces were between fifteen and twenty miles from the city. Four days later when Russian and American troops met on the Elbe, Berlin was surrounded, the districts of Zehlendorf and Dahlem falling on the 26th followed by Gatow airfield, Spandau and Neuköln on the next.

In the early hours of 29th April, Hitler married his mistress Eva Braun, then after a champagne breakfast, he dictated his will and political testament before appointing Grand Admiral Dönitz as his successor and attending his last war conference where the Commandant of Berlin, General Weidling reported that Russian troops were about three hundred metres from the bunker. Weidling suggested forming a battle group to attempt a break-out but Hitler said that he himself, would stay in Berlin.

The following day Hitler shot himself, and his wife took poison. Their bodies were carried out of the bunker, laid in a foundation trench in the Chancellery garden, doused with petrol and burned.

On 4 May German forces in north-western Germany surrendered to Montgomery. Dönitz had wanted to end the war in the west but continue the fight against the Russians but his proposal was rejected. The Germans signed an unconditional surrender at 2.41am on 7th May at Eisenhower's headquarters. Winston Churchill announced victory to the House of Commons on the following afternoon.

Though the war was officially over, the fighting continued in Czechoslovakia until the 13th and in Yugoslavia until the 15th. Behind the Russian lines some German units fought their way to the West, others in remote areas had no one to whom they could formally surrender. The U-boat bases of Lorient, St Nazaire, La Rochelle and La Palisse did not surrender until the 9th and one U-boat, U-977, did not surrender until three months later when it arrived at Rio de la Plata in Argentina.

In the Far East the Japanese fought fanatically for every inch of territory and it seemed that the war there would drag on into 1946. A direct assault on the Japanese mainland was expected to cost 800,000 Allied lives. On 6 August, Hiroshima was destroyed by an atomic bomb. Three days later, a second bomb was dropped, this time the city of Nagasaki was the target. On 14 August, the Japanese Government accepted unconditional surrender, the formal capitulation being signed on board the American battleship *Missouri* in Tokyo Bay on 2 September.

The Second World War was over.

Some of the huge crowd that thronged Whitehall to hear Winston Churchill's speech celebrate at the news that Germany had capitulated.

Whitehall, London. It's party time for this RAF officer, two members of the Women's Auxiliary Air Force and a civilian.

On one of the lions in Trafalgar Square. Victory signs from RT Westall and RD Dowes of the US Navy, G Yoke of the US Army and Harry Armstrong from Perth, Australia. Are the two on the left trying to tell the cameraman something?

The Royal Family, with Winston Churchill, acknowledging the vast crowds that gathered outside
Buckingham Palace.

The crowd cheer and wave. On the balcony are their Majesties with the Princesses Elizabeth
and Margaret Rose.

"Roll out the barrel". A lorry load of beer trundles through Piccadilly.

Just one of thousands of street parties held. This one was at Kentwell Close, Brockley.

Victory tea party and concert in Wimbledon.

Ginger and Little Mickey, clowns with Trevor's Circus, toured LCC parks giving shows for youngsters.

It's demob day! *Above:* Royal Artillery troops at No 4 Military Collecting Unit, Duke of York Headquarters, Chelsea. *Left:* Chief Petty Officer Arthur Hime of Copenhagen Street, Islington, receives his discharge at Chatham after 43 years of service. *Below:* Wrens receive their clothing coupons and money at the pay office. A week after VE Day a Government announcement stated that by the end of 1945 around 750,000 service personnel would be demobbed.

Japan surrenders. The crowd celebrate and the policeman who tried to get the traffic moving gets cheered and chaired.

A member of the Chinese Military Mission complete with inscrutable smile.

The King receives the nation's leaders at the palace. *Left to right:* Admiral of the Fleet, Sir Andrew Cunningham; Lord President of the Council, Herbert Morrison; Secretary of the War Cabinet, Sir Edward Bridges; the Prime Minister, Clement Atlee; Chief of Staff to the Minister of Defence, Sir Hastings Ismay; His Majesty King George VI; Chief of the Air Staff, Sir Charles Portal; the Lord Privy Seal, Arthur Greenwood; the First Lord of the Admiralty, AV Alexander; Chief of the Imperial Staff, Field Marshal Sir Alan Brooke; Secretary of State for Foreign Affairs, Ernest Bevin.

Buckingham Palace floodlit for VJ night.

VJ night celebrations in Trafalgar Square.

VJ night celebrations on Clapham Common.

Victory Day celebrations, June 1946. The Household Cavalry escort the Royal landau along
Oxford Street.

Members of the United States contingent approach the saluting base.

Mohammed Ali Mowallu was
one of the members of the
Transjordan contingent.

The Women's Land Army contingent in Oxford Street.

Cromwell tanks lower their guns in salute as they pass the saluting base as part of the Victory Day
mechanized column.

Here we go again . . . or do we? To commemorate the momentous acts of the summer of 1940, the RAF restaged scenes from the Battle of Britain for the television cameras in September 1946. The pilots are shown waiting at ten minute readiness for the order to "scramble!" at RAF Biggin Hill. The aircraft are Spitfire LFI6Es, powered by licence-built Merlin engines manufactured by the American firm Packard. Had they been lined up like this in 1940, chances are that the *Luftwaffe* would have made short work of them.